The Words of the Day
The Unlikely Evolution of Common English

Steven M. Cerutti, Ph.D.

This book is dedicated to her for whom there exist the Words of the Night...

The Words of the Day
The Unlikely Evolution of Common English
By Steven M. Cerutti, Ph.D.

Printed in the United States of America.

Published in Kittrell, North Carolina, USA.

Academic Series: Book # 1

Series Editor: Don Burleson

Editors: Robin Haden, and Janet Burleson

Production Editor: Janet Burleson

Cover Design: Bryan Hoff

Illustrations: Joel White

Printing History:

      December 2005 for First Edition

ISBN: 0-9761573-3-0

Library of Congress Control Number: 2005928020

Acknowledgements

ad • gnoscere: (Latin: *ad* ("toward") + *gnoscere* ('to know, recognize) + the old English suffix "laec" > "ledge" + the grammatical suffix "ment" which makes it into a noun. Literally, "the act of showing recognition toward someone or something."

This project was not feasible without the help from some key individuals. And I would like to take this opportunity to thank them. Don Burleson, the publisher and series editor, for having faith in a first time author and providing useful insight in the book writing process. Thanks Don!

Special thanks are due to Christina Eftekharzadeh, without whose editorial guidance this book would not have been possible, and my illustrator, Joel White, who brought my words to life. Finally, special thanks are due to the many students over the years who attended my "Greek and Latin for Vocabulary Building" course, who dragged their asses into classes every week at 9 a.m., who laughed at my corny jokes, listened to my long-winded stories, and, hopefully, learned to love words a little bit.

Steven M. Cerutti
East Carolina University

The following stories are true. Some of the names have been changed to protect the ignorant.

Foreword

To most people, the Foreword is the part of the book you skip, and most people do, me included. Or at least I did until I got paid to write a few, and then I sort of felt obligated to read a few. Now I kind of like them, as they tend to be short, interesting stories. Ironically, perhaps we should call our Foreword a Backword, since, as in many places in this book, we'll be traveling back in time to dig up the roots of the words we use every day.

Back in England, in the bad old days of Knights and Kings and Lords and Ladies, back when round tables were all the rage and every castle had to have one, there was this guy called King Edward II (it was about 1377, but let's not get our pantaloons all in a knot over dates, just know it was sometime after Edward I and before Edward III). He must have been held back in the second grade for "not playing well with others," or maybe he had his milk money stolen too many times, but once he became king it was obvious he had some old scores to settle and that "heads were going to roll." Literally.

Edward chose a spot on the northwest slope of the marshy hill surrounding the Tower of London. They called the spot the Tower Green because it was on a grassy rise overlooking both the Tower on the river side and a large gently sloping hill that approached it from the north, affording it great visibility (even Edward knew: location, location, location!). It was on this spot that the king ordered to be built a small platform of wooden scaffolding with a single set of stairs on one side leading one way — up.

Talk, Talk, Talk

A criminal was tried in Parliament, a large, austere palatial building up river from the Tower. The root of the word "Parliament" is, of course from the French *parlare*, which means to talk (which is odd, since at this point the English and the French for the most part hated each other). They still do it there today. Talk, I mean. And I mean a lot of it. Today, it is the seat of the British government and trials are not held there anymore, but back in the days of old Eddie the Second they indeed were, and this is where the word gets its primary meaning, because this is where charges brought against individuals by the state were announced, where testimony was given, where verdicts delivered. A lot of talking involved in all that, but despite what the defense had to say, they were all convicted. England has a brutal history.

Not Your Average Pleasure Cruise

After the accused was convicted, he was put in a little boat, rowed down the Thames to the Tower. On the way, they would have to pass under London Bridge and the last sight the condemned man would see as he passed under the bridge and approached the "Traitor's Gate" that would lead him into the Tower was what his final fate would be. Mounted on pikes all across the top of London Bridge were the rotting heads of those who had recently visited Tower Green, and upon many of these rotting skulls perched the famous Tower Ravens (no, not the Royal Rugby team), great black, shiny birds, big as eagles, feeding off the flesh of the decapitations.

Welcome to London

Not your Average Bed & Breakfast

Some people stayed in the Tower for just a few days, some for years. But when the day came the condemned man (or woman) was marched out of the Tower and up Tower Green before cheering crowds. As he approached the scaffolding with the single set of stairs he looked up and saw, awaiting him at the top, the executioner—a large, dark, hooded figure with two axes in his meaty palms: one sharp, one dull. And as the condemned man climbed that stairway and mounted the

platform he would hand the executioner, if he could, a sack of coins—
he certainly wasn't going to need them where he was going!

You get what you pay for... "tipping" for good service.

And the executioner would put the sack on a set of scales and if it
tipped the scales, he would use the sharp axe, and if it didn't, he would
use the dull one. Most of the people watching booed if the sack of
coins tipped the scales because they preferred to watch head whacking
done with the dull axe, as it usually took several swings to get the head
off—which mean more blood and screaming—always a crowd pleaser.
I mean what's the fun of watching a man lose his head in one clean,
painless, blow? As legend has it, the sack of coins that the condemned
handed to the executioner was known as "severance pay," and the idea
of whether or not it "tipped" the scale is where we get our expression

of "tipping" for good service." That story was told to me when I was ten years old while actually taking a tour of the Tower of London and I have been fascinated with words ever since.

Introduction

In the spring of 1992 I graduated from Duke University with a Doctorate in Classics. Then I was offered a job at East Carolina University. They wanted me to start a Classical Studies program. The university had just undergone a review by the Carnegie Foundation and had been told that if it indeed wanted to get a chapter of Phi Beta Kappa on campus (and believe me, it did), then East Carolina would have to have a substantial Classical Studies program, one which offered not just Latin (which was already taught there, but just barely), but also ancient Greek, as well as a full complement of courses in translation. So the combination of these two events prompted the Dean of the College of Arts & Sciences to do what all deans do when events converge: he formed a committee, a committee to hire a "Classicist." From what I could gather during my interview, no one on that committee really knew the difference between a "Classicist" and a panda bear. What they did know, I think, was that the individual they were looking for to start this all important new program in Classics was going to have to be someone sharp and sharp-witted, vivacious, youthful, good looking, creative, energetic, innovative, a charmer, someone who could sell snow to the Eskimos if he had to and even if he didn't.

But they got me instead.

Monday Morning Wake-Up Call

My first Latin class at East Carolina. It was the fall semester of 1992 and I had a 10 AM section of first-level students, new to the language, new to the college, and at noon a group of third-level students I'd inherited from the previous occupier of my position, whose decision to retire coincided conveniently with my arrival. Twelve students in all. Two Latin classes and twelve students. Not much to work with, but I got to work all the same.

Writing a Classics Curriculum

I needed a curriculum. So I spent the first semester thinking up some good old standard Classics courses, turning them into course proposals, and then single-handedly, walking them up through the chain of committees all the way from the College of Arts & Sciences, to the Faculty Senate, to the Office of the Chancellor. What they all were thinking as I prattled on I have no idea. I wrote, and passed, all told, sixteen course proposals that first semester.

When I was finished, there was the seminar in Cicero's letters, the "Age of Augustus," there was "Women in Antiquity," and the old standby (and one of my personal favorites), "Greek Tragedy in Translation." Now there were upper-level courses in Latin, and low and behold, a full load of the language of the ancient Greeks from the first year to the fourth. Hell, I was knee deep in course names and numbers.

It was somewhere near mid semester when I noticed that no one was registering for these courses. Then it struck me. What I had created was a curriculum. But that was all it was. A framework. A Template. Was one of my twelve (actually by then it had dwindled down to eight) Latin students—most of whom were business majors and taking Latin because of the university's two-year foreign language requirement, and because taking Latin meant they didn't have to sit in the language lab three hours a week, as they would have had they taken a modern language like Spanish or French—were *they* going to start suddenly taking an interest in ancient Greek, or Greek Tragedy in Translation? I needed one more class, something that would draw the students in, get them excited about Classics—if not explain to them what "Classics" was to begin with.

The "Word of the Day"

I called the class "Greek and Latin for Vocabulary Building." I chose a text, but the textbook was not important. I knew what I was going to do. What I did was, every day I began class by writing a "Word of the Day" on the board. Some carefully chosen word that usually everyone in the class knew and thought they knew the meaning of, some word that might also wake them up, get their attention.

And then, after a few timid attempts at defining the word by a few brave students, I'd whip out the axe and sever them from their own ignorance, revealing what the word "*means* means." I'd do this by telling them a story as compelling as the Beefeater's—only my stock was not the brutal history of the British Monarchy, but the Rome of the Caesars, which is just as full of horrifying, shocking, hilarious, sexy, naughty, bawdy, and downright dirty stories that explain where some of our most common words come from.

With each "Word of the Day" I began infusing the students with knowledge of ancient Greece and Rome—of Classics. The first time I taught the course, it had, predictably, only about nineteen students in it. I mean the title "Greek and Latin for Vocabulary Building" is hardly the sexy beast that's going to pull them in in droves. But the *words*. And the stories behind them—that's what did it.

And as I got better at it, as I began to refine my selection of which words I would use for my "Word of the Day," as I got better at telling the stories, something began to happen. The "Words of the Day" began to take on a life of their own. "Cerutti's Word of the Day" began to be, or so I heard, posted daily on the bulletin board in the Sigma Sigma Sigma Sorority House. Somebody, I was told, started a "Word of the Day" website. Within two semesters, "word of mouth," that most powerful tool in advertising, sent my course into the stratosphere.

In order to accommodate the rising number of students who wanted to take it, the course had to be moved into the largest lecture hall on campus, and even after opening a second section, there was still a waiting list. The next thing I knew it had been voted "Most Popular Class on Campus" by a poll conducted by the student newspaper. Not only did the success of this course increase its own enrollments, it created a trickle-down effect so that seats began to fill in ancient Greek and the courses in translation. The success of the vocabulary course allowed me to further broaden the scope of the Classics curriculum; I started adding slide lecture courses on ancient Rome (my other specialty) and Pompeii. These, too, filled to capacity the largest lecture halls on campus.

When I arrived at East Carolina in 1992 I was the only Classicist here with 12 students and two sections of Latin. Today, we have four tenured or tenure-track people and two full-time instructors. We offer 12 courses each semester with a combined enrollment of nearly 600 students. Not bad, huh?

The Words of the Day

What follows are, simply a selection of the now famous "Words of the Day." Obviously, over the years, they have changed, come and gone and come back again. But these are the ones that jump-started Classics at East Carolina University. Oh, I switch them around from semester to semester, but in the pages that follow are some of the biggest, baddest, bare-assed words that come into English from Latin and Greek. For the most part, the criteria I use for my "Words of the Day" are:

They should be words that the students have already heard before

They have to sometimes be provocative (it is, after all, a 9 AM class!)

They have to sometimes not be provocative (one must pace oneself!)

They have to be grounded in the Greek of Plato and Socrates, and the Latin of Cicero and the Caesars

And, most importantly, they have to have interesting stories behind them

The words discussed in the chapters that follow do not occur in the same order in which I usually present them when I teach the course. The format of a book is necessarily different from that of a college classroom. To address this problem I have grouped the words into chapters where a series of words may share a common root, or follow a particular theme. This, too, is a fine way to approach the subject.

Enjoy!

The Words of Today and Yesterday

Mixology

It's All in the Ingredients

Great chefs the world over will tell you that the most important thing in the preparation of great meals is having the proper ingredients. Painters feel the same way about their pigments and brushes, as do sculptors about their stone.

They say Michaelangelo spent six months combing the quarries of Carrara in northern Italy in search of that perfect chunk of marble from which he would carve his *Pietà*. Six months may seem like a long time to pick out a rock (at least that's what he told his *wife* he was doing!), but the *Pietà*, on view in St. Peter's Basilica in Rome, is regarded as his greatest achievement in stone. In fact it might be greater even perhaps than the *David*—which is saying something, seeing as he also sculpted the *Pietà* at the age of seventeen. In other words, what you end up with depends on what you start out with.

A Rosé By Any Other Name…

Say you went into a bar and ordered a glass of Rosé and they brought you a glass of Merlot? Better yet, what if you ordered a Gin & Tonic? You would expect to get a glass full of just that: gin and tonic. Not whisky and sour mix—that's called a Whisky Sour.

Most things have names based on what they're made of. Too bad the rest of the world isn't as clearly defined. But clarity *can* be found in words. Words have meaning and in order to understand a word's true meaning, we first must break it down into its original ingredients. Not necessarily how it is used—God knows how people misuse, mistreat, and misappropriate words—but to understand what a word *means*, you have to cut it open and look inside. One last analogy: if someone placed before you two cakes and asked you which one had nuts in it and which did not, you would only be guessing unless you cut them open and looked inside

Romancing the Romans

Words come into English from almost every language on the globe—many still spoken today, many not. For our purposes, we will examine, for the most part, words that derive their meanings from the ancient tongues of the Romans and Greeks.

We must understand that first and foremost the meaning of a word is based on its "root"—that is, on that part of the word that comes directly into English from a Latin or ancient Greek word. Why? Because long ago, everyone living from Scotland to what is modern day Iraq was part of the former Roman Empire and therefore spoke Latin (and many of the highly educated among them also still knew their ancient Greek!). As time went on, different dialects began emerging in different regions as the former Roman Empire turned into what would become modern Europe. These regions turned into countries, and their dialects became their languages. We refer to these as the "Romance Languages" not because women tend to swoon whenever you look deep into their eyes and utter something like *mi amor* or *je t'aime*, but because of their Roman heritage. These countries are generally considered to be Italy, Spain, and France, which is why their languages are all so similar.

Digging up our Roots

Understanding a word in English involves first identifying its Latin or Greek root. Once we've done that, we're good to go—that is, we've got our *root*, but we do not yet have a *word*. In order to turn a *root* into a *word* in English, we need to add an ending, or "suffix," which will determine what part of speech, such as noun, verb, adjective, adverb, etc., we have made. We might then want to add something in front of the root, called a "prefix." These little elements are very simple, but very important and can have a significant effect on the final meaning of a word because they often deal with motion and show direction, such as up, down, in, out, over, under, etc.

Learning to Say "No"

Some people have a hard time saying "No." But if you've got your Latin and Greek prefixes in order, it's really no problem because that's another important aspect of the prefix. It has the power to say "No," to the root of the word. In Latin, these *negators* are *un* and *in*, and they can be found, for example, in words like *unalterable* (*un • alter • able*) or *insensitive* (*in • sensi • tive*). Ancient Greek has only one *negatory* prefix, the single letter alpha (α). But since we use the Roman alphabet and not the Greek alphabet, α transliterates into our letter *a* and appears in words such as *amoral* (*a • mor • al*) or *atypical* (*a • typic • al*). This *negatory* use of the alpha is referred to by linguists as the *Alpha Privative* because it "deprives" the root of its meaning. That's a very fancy name for a very simple concept, but it's sure to impress people at cocktail parties and might even get you laid—which was the whole reason why language was probably invented in the first place, right? We'll revisit this topic—negating words, that is—in a later chapter.

Putting it all Together

It's really quite straightforward. All words in English fit into a very simple "template." Once you separate the root from the prefix and the suffix, you're home free!

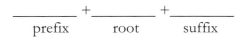

Ready to have some fun? Turn to the next chapter, where we'll play with some roots, prefixes and suffixes. You'll see the potential of mastering the many possibilities that words have once you understand them and experience the sense of empowerment that comes with being able to control words, instead of always feeling like words control you.

Word Power

Family Values

In ancient Rome, due to the high mortality rate not just among the adult population—which was high enough—but particularly among young children, a family's best and often only chance of having at least one son survive into adulthood to carry on the family name was to have as many children as possible and hope most of them were male. With a little luck, you would be blessed with a boy; a lotta luck got you a bunch of boys.

The Roman goddess of luck was named Fortuna, and you can bet pregnant women, as well as those trying to get pregnant, probably spent many hours praying at her shrines and temples on a daily basis for a masculine child to drop out of their wombs.

 Archaeological Note: The goddess Fortuna had at least twenty-eight temples and sanctuaries in and around Rome—that we know of, at least. That should tell you *something*!

Boys Will Be Boys

Let's face it: the odds were not in your favor in those days. First of all, it was highly likely that if you were fortunate enough to have a son, the odds were something like one in three that he (or his mother, or both) would die in childbirth. If he escaped that fate, there was always the chance that some subsequent illness to which infants are particularly prone would rob you of your heir. If he made it into his adolescent years, there was always the danger that junior might wander into his parents' bedroom and find Dad's sword in the back of his underwear drawer and decide to show it off to the kid next door while they were playing "Gladiator." The next thing you know, he's become just another statistic. Or he could get hit by a chariot just crossing the street! Finally, if the young man managed to make it to the age of, say, eighteen, there was always military service— required of all young men of aristocratic birth—where he could easily enough find himself playing "Catch the Spear" without a mitt during training exercises or inadvertently swallow an arrow on the battlefield. And given the state of the medical profession back then—*state*? hell, it wouldn't even have qualified as a *territory*—even the slightest of flesh wounds could quickly become infected and, since this was before the advent of antibiotics, it would be *game over*.

Daughters: The Down Side

Girls married very young—often as early as twelve or thirteen. This was common practice in order to squeeze the maximum yield of childbearing years out of them. Making babies—especially *boy* babies— was important, so if your new bride could not produce sons, it was grounds for immediate and uncontested divorce, in which case the young girl would be returned to her family probably never to marry again. Because once word got round as to why she was divorced, no one else would want to marry her. What would be the point?

So, by the age of, say, fifteen, the poor girl's life would essentially be over. She would live out her days as a shadowy figure lurking about the family household, an unwanted burden, doing what she could to help out. This meant a life of weaving and working the loom, milking the cows—or if the father so chose, and he had every right to do so under Roman law and often did—"milking" Dad's "friends" in the back room for a few *sesterces* a pop (a *sestertius* was the equivalent of about a buck). The poor girl had few options left, so if that meant earning her keep on her knees (or her back), so be it. This is particularly ironic since today we know that it is the male who determines the sex of the child. The woman has nothing to do with it!

Daughters: The Up Side

On the other hand, because of the importance of having sons, a young girl who could produce male children was a commodity in great demand. There was a big market for these creatures. A daughter who could produce heirs was the goose that could lay the golden egg! A daughter such as this allowed a shrewd father, who had arranged a marriage for his daughter with the son of a more prestigious and politically powerful family, to cash in on that marriage big time!

Just as they are today, marriages in ancient Rome were legal contracts. Once two families were joined through marriage, the political contacts and inroads enjoyed by the more powerfully connected family of the groom suddenly became open to the family of the bride. But of course, being a virgin and untested, if the young girl failed to produce, all bets were off.

Congratulations, *Est Puer*!

It must have been pure hell, that first year, for the family of the bride. More than likely, the stress could span the first two or three years, as I'm sure if the first child were a girl, they would try again. And again. All this time the family of the bride (remember, this was before ultra sound testing) would be waiting to hear the words that would guarantee their family's elevated social status: "Congratulations, it's a boy!"

Hearing these words was the object of the game. It meant that the newlywed couple would have at least one son—and if she could have *one* son, she could have *another*...and *another*...and *another*. The more sons, the more powerful the family. Since those sons were also related by blood to the family of the bride, both sides made out. This was how Roman society worked—among the upper class at least (and who cared about anyone else?). Marriage and politics were inseparable pursuits.

Marriage and Politics

Things aren't so different today. If you notice, most powerful families in today's politically charged, highly competitive world are large, and have lots of boys. I'm thinking of families like the Rockefellers, the Kennedys—even the current First Family can boast of two presidents and a governor. Political power has always been associated with big families dominated by males.

Getting at the Root of Power

The root of our word "power" comes from the Latin adjective *potens*, meaning "powerful." The root of *potens* is *pot*, so this will be the root of any words we make in English having to do with power. If we were to plug the root, *pot*, into our template, it would look like this:

$$\underset{\text{PREFIX}}{\underline{\hspace{3cm}}} \quad + \quad \underset{\text{ROOT}}{pot} \quad + \quad \underset{\text{SUFFIX}}{\underline{\hspace{3cm}}}$$

Now *pot* is not yet a word (unless you're talking about the kind you cook with, put flowers in, or smoke!), it's still just a *root* that means "power." In order to make it a word, we first have to stick a suffix onto it, remember? There are many from which to choose, and whichever one we do choose will determine whether we make a noun, adjective, verb, etc. For example, if we add *–ent* onto the root, we get the word *potent* (*pot • ent*), an adjective which means having the quality or characteristic *(–ent)* of power *(pot)*. If we added *–ency* to the end of *pot,* we would get *potency* (*pot • ency*), a noun meaning power.

All Power Is Fleeting

It's a dog-eat-dog world out there, and whenever someone gets a little power, there's always someone else who wants to take it away. Things can, and usually do, get personal. While this "negativity" does exist in the world of words, you can relax, as words don't take things personally. If you want to take the *power* away from the word *potency,* we would simply add a negatory prefix. Since we're dealing with a Latin root *(pot),* we would add the Latin prefix *in* onto the front of it:

$$in \quad + \quad pot \quad + \quad ency$$
PREFIX   ROOT   SUFFIX

Because the way we spell words is often affected by the way we pronounce them, when you start splicing prefixes and suffixes onto roots, funky changes can occur in the spelling of the final product. If we connected the three elements in our template above, we would get the word *inpotency.* The correct spelling of the word, however, is *impotency.* What happens is that often when a prefix that ends in a consonant (in this case the letter *n*), collides with a root that begins with a consonant (in this case the letter *p*), the *n* of the prefix often changes to an *m.* I say often because this doesn't always happen, and as is often the case with compound words, there are no real rules to dictate when it will and when it won't. Most times, though, it *does* happen, and there are many examples of it—the words *imposter* or *impossible* are a couple of examples—but then there's always the exception to the rule, such as the words incapacitated or *input,* etc. (for further discussion on this see Chapter Five, "When Consonants Collide").

> **Historical Note:** The emperor Caligula's horse was named *Incitatus.* Since the Latin adverb *cito* means "quickly," the prefix in probably just intensifies (but it *doesn't* change—when you're the emperor's horse, you don't have to follow the rules!—his name probably best translates into something like "Speed Racer." It wasn't long before Caligula, who was quite fond of his horse, made it "Senator Speed Racer."

The Real "Root" of Power

Okay, so if the word *impotence* literally means *having no power,* then how has it come to be a euphemism in our common vernacular for what your doctor today would call *erectile dysfunction*, but what we all know simply and sadly as meaning you can't "get it up?"

What do *power* and a "stiff prick" have to do with one another? Do you have to lift weights in order to get a "hard-on?" Is there a connection between political clout and "sporting a woody?" Well, if having lots of sons was the ticket to the successful continuation of the family name and many sons increased the odds of political advancement for that family, the burden ultimately did not rest entirely on the woman's ability to produce them. Because before she could even begin to do her part, the male participant in the erotic ritual had to be able to do his. In the simplest of terms, no "cheese dick" was ever going to rule the Roman Empire—in fact, if the ancient Romans had Viagra, we'd all still be wearing togas and speaking Latin!

The Real "F" Word

No, It's Not What You're Thinking

It's what you're *saying*. Sorry, but this chapter isn't about *that* "F" word. That will come later. This chapter concerns a different "F" word. It's about a root, actually: the root *fa*. *Fa* is one of the oldest and most important roots that we have. In fact, if we didn't have it, we probably wouldn't be around to get our rocks off doing the *other* "F" word. The root *fa* goes all the way back to the ancient Greek root φη which transliterates into Latin, as well as English, as both *pha* and *fa*.

Food for Thought

Both *fa* and *pha* have to do with anything that goes in or out of your mouth. It can be food, words—even body parts. I'm talking the bare essentials here, and we'll get to those in more detail in the next chapter. For now, we'll concentrate on the most common aspects of *fa* and *pha* and what most Americans spend the most time doing anyway: eating and talking.

The Romans were for the most part vegetarians. They only ate meat on festival days when the Pontifex Maximus, the High Priest of Rome, performed a public sacrifice, usually involving the slaughter of some variety of edible livestock. After the sacrificial victim was killed and disemboweled, only a small portion of the animal's entrails—usually the liver—was burned on an altar as an offering to the god in whose name the festival was dedicated. The rest of the animal was cooked over a large spit and everyone enjoyed what amounted to a free Bar-B-Q dinner—a huge pig-pickin' for all who showed up. And *all* did!

What Romans usually ate for their daily subsistence was a kind gruel that consisted of corn meal, wheat, and oats. They called this meal *far*. It was carried down into their stomachs through their eso*pha*gus—both words sharing the same root. Incidentally, the root *fa* is also where our word "family" comes from. This is a little ironic, since in most families anyway, when everyone gets together to eat, nobody's ever got much of anything to say to anybody.

Better Watch What You Say...

The ancient Romans didn't believe in the concept of a predetermined "destiny." They believed that a man created his own fate in a very particular way, and it all goes back to the root *fa*. This is how it worked: from the moment someone is born, he is *infans*, the Latin adjective from which our word "infant" is derived. If we break the word down into its ingredients, we see that it fits our standard template of prefix + root + suffix (*in* • *fa* • *nt*). According to its ingredients, the word "infant" means "someone or something that cannot *fa*." Notice how it has nothing to do with age, size, weight or any of those other ways people misuse this word.

Now, how you interpret the root *fa* in the context of the word "infant" is where the study of word origins gets interesting, because an "infant" can neither speak nor feed himself. In this case, the *fa* in "infant" probably cuts both ways, but if I had to come down on one side or the other, I'd say the ancient Romans used the root *fa* in *infans* primarily to describe the fact that the child had not yet learned to speak.

> **Comical Aside:** This would be the perfect opportunity to make a joke about the fact that the poor kid was going to have to learn to *speak* Latin, and that for students today, just learning to *read* Latin involves some pretty tough sledding as it is, but I just can't come up with one.

Now, as the child grows up and learns to speak, something important happens. It happens to all of us, actually, whether we're speaking Latin or not. As you advance through infancy into adolescence and adulthood, you find out pretty fast that the words you say have meaning and that you have to take responsibility for the things that come out of your mouth. In other words, if you say you're going to do something, then *dammit*, you have *to do* what you *said* you'd do.

In Latin, the root of the verb *to do* is *fac/fact* (from the verb *facere*). Now you don't have to have a Ph.D. in Linguistics to grasp that the root *fac/fact* ("to do") contains within it a smaller ingredient, a pinch so to speak, of the root *fa* ("to speak"). You also don't have to be a genius—hell, living in the world for a few hours would probably do the trick—to understand that words lead to action, and that there are consequences to what comes out of your mouth.

Better Watch What Others say...

Now, if you're the type of person who is true to his word, who does what he says he'll do, then people will tend to say good things about you—that you're a stand-up sort of guy, all that sort of stuff. But if you're out there in the world, talking all kinds of shit, not following through on promises, then people will be talking you down.

You see, the ancient Greeks and Romans lived in what's referred to as a "shame culture," whereas, we today live in a "guilt culture." Back in the days of the Trojan War, for example, if Achilles—the fiercest, deadliest, most dangerous of all the Greek warriors—if he went out and killed a bunch of Trojans, maybe even slit their throats while they slept in the night, and everyone cheered and said, "Great job, Achilles, way to go!" old Achilles, he'd feel pretty good about himself. He would only feel bad if his behavior elicited an opposite response: one that made him feel bad, that "shamed" him in the eyes of his fellow warriors.

We, on the other hand, in our modern culture would tend to feel bad about ourselves if we went out and slit the throats of a bunch of people while they slept—even in warfare. Well…let's hope that's true for most of us, anyway. That's because modern society is mostly based on a "guilt culture." Guilt comes from within ourselves, based on how we feel about our own behavior. Shame comes from outside us, from what others think or say about our behavior.

Famous, Like Achilles

So then, if you lived up to your *fa*—if you were "true to your word" as the expression goes, then you got a good *fama*. If you did not, you got a bad *fama*. Our word "fame" derives from this Latin noun, and it means what people say about you. "Good Achilles, atta boy!" And Achilles feels good about himself. "Bad Achilles, bad boy!" And Achilles' self esteem goes south for the winter. It doesn't bother him if he slaughters a hundred men in a single, murderous rampage, just so long as it doesn't bother anybody else.

For most of us, I think such behavior would become somewhat problematic in our lives. The Post Traumatic Stress Disorder that many soldiers experience, particularly if they saw a lot of action, is a good example of the difference between the *shame* and *guilt* cultures.

I am sure Achilles would not have had any problem re-adjusting to ancient Greek life when he returned to Phthia (pronounced *ph-thee-ah*), his home town, after the war. I am sure he would not have experienced bad dreams, had flashbacks, required therapy, or been put on mood medications like many of the American veterans, particularly those who came back from the conflict in Vietnam. No, because Achilles would return home with a good *fama* with him, which would insure that a good *fata* awaited him as well.

From the Cradle to the Grave

Our word *fate*, which derives from the Latin noun *fata*, also shares the root *fa*. Your *fata*, or *fate* was what happened to you at the end of your life but only as a direct result of your *fama*. You are born *infans*. As you begin to grow and learn to speak, you develop a *fama* which, ultimately, will determine your *fata*. Achilles had a great *fama* and would have enjoyed a wonderful *fata* back in Phthia had he not been shot in his heel with an arrow by that wimpy, panty-waist, pussy-whipped Paris, who started the whole war when he stole Helen from Sparta.

> **Mythological Note:** Achilles' mother was a sea nymph named Thetis who, before her son went off to war, dunked his body into the river Styx in the underworld, which put a kind of protective coating all over him so he could not be wounded. She held onto him by his heel, so his heel did not get the protective coating, thus it was the one spot where he was vulnerable. This is the origin of our expression *Achilles heel* when referring to someone's weak spot.

So, even a good *fama* will not protect you from a well-aimed arrow a bad *fama* can kill you just as fast. There was another warrior back in the days of Troy, and his name was Ajax. One night Ajax had a little too much of the old vino, got trashed, and went out and slaughtered a bunch of his fellow Greeks as they slept, thinking he was slaughtering sheep. In the morning, when he came to his senses, he realized what he had done.

The problem was, so did everybody else in the camp. "Bad Ajax!" they shouted, "Bad! Bad!" He was so shamed by this *fama* that he threw himself on his sword. As goes one's *fama*, so goes one's *fata*, as they say. So you see, from the cradle to the grave, the root *fa* tracks every move throughout your life. The ancient Greeks and Romans felt strongly about language and taking responsibility for what you say, how the things you say lead to the things you end up having to do, and how the things you do lead to what happens to you at the end of your life. Nothing could be more true, even today.

> **Historical Note:** Seeing as we have been covering war a bit in this chapter, I'll bet you never thought about the relationship between the words *infant* and *infantry*. Obviously they are related through the shared root *fa*. There is a reason why infantry soldiers, particularly during the Vietnam era, referred to themselves as *grunts*. While the particular expressions and terminology may differ from generation to generation, one thing remains the same, and that is if you end up in the *infantry*, no one cares what you have to *say*, and you are expected to do what you are told. This actually dates back to the medieval era. When knights would go into battle, they rode in on horseback; however, they needed help with their armor. Once in the armor, they needed help getting on the horse, and when they were done fighting, they would need help getting out of the armor. As a result, they were usually accompanied by one of their serfs or servants on foot, whose job it was to help out with the details like that. Because most knights were also Lords, or some kind of royalty, their servants were expected not to speak unless spoken to. When the going got tough, they sometimes had to join in the fighting. These people were referred to as the "infantry" because they were expected to keep their mouths shut; however, the word as it is used today refers to the fact that these men were the earliest form of foot soldiers, even though the word has nothing to do with feet, walking or soldiering.

Controlling Your Vowel Movements

Vowel Surfing

So there you are again, sitting in front of the tube, remote in hand, surfing around for a show on the *Lost Land of the Mayans* that you heard was airing on the "Archaeology" Channel. But when you get there, you see that it is actually on the "Archeology" Channel. Despite the difference in spelling, I doubt you missed the show.

You probably even learned something—and not just about ancient Mayan rituals and culture. Maybe you noticed along the way that there is very little difference in the pronunciation of the vowel "e" and the diphthong "ae" as they appear in the words "archeology" and "archaeology." This is because the root of both words is from the Greek adjective *archaios* (say: "ar-keye-ohs"), meaning "old" or "ancient." When we transliterate the Greek letters into Roman characters, the diphthong "ai" comes into English as either "e" or "ae."

> **Linguistic Note:** Unfortunately, a "diphthong" is not something you order out of a Victoria's Secret catalogue; rather, a diphthong is two vowels that combine to make a single sound, such as "ou," "au," "eu," or "oi," to name some of the most common ones.

The First Words Were *Spoken*

And God said, "Let there be light!" God *said*. He didn't put it in a memo or send it in an e-mail, right? That's because long before people began writing them down, words existed, and people used them orally. Words began as the grunts and noises we made to try to express to each other certain ideas, like "Hey, watch out for that mountain lion!" Once people got around to developing a way of transferring these sounds into symbols, though, it was, at first, for not nearly as exciting stuff.

Not Nearly as Exciting Stuff

Doing the laundry is not nearly as exciting as dodging mountain lions, but this seems to have been the subject of our earliest written documents. Indeed, the earliest fragments that we have of formal writing are inventories, laundry lists.

Vowel Variety: The Splice of Life

If you've ever gone in search of a "laundramat" and found instead a "laundromat," I will bet you still got the wash done. The word is a combination of *laundr* (whose root comes into English after a brief *tour de France* from the Latin verb *lavare*, meaning "to wash") plus "mat," which completes the root as a noun ("mat" is an abbreviation of the Greek suffix "matic," which describes something that works automatically.)

When we splice roots that end in consonants with suffixes that begin with them, we English speakers tend to insert a vowel between them to make the final product easier to pronounce. Most of the time, we use the letter "o," but since "o" is only one of six vowel choices, there is a lot of latitude here with the other vowels. This is why there is so much variation in how many words are spelled, especially when it comes to their vowels. I mean, it would be a pretty boring world if the only vowel we had was "o," would it not?

Let's try a little experiment. I am going to splice the root "laundr" and the suffix "mat" together using all the vowels in the English language.

LAUNDRAMAT

LAUNDREMAT

LAUNDRIMAT
LAUNDROMAT
LAUNDRUMAT
LAUNDRYMAT

There's a laundry list for you! Now, say each one out loud—*laundramat, laundremat, laundrimat, laundromat, laundrumat,* and (sometimes) *laundrymat.* Any real difference in the way they sound? No. Not really. The reason is that, linguistically speaking, vowels are weak things. So weak, in fact, that there are many languages—some still spoken today—that do not use any vowels whatsoever and everybody still plays "Dodge the Mountain Lion" and gets the wash done just fine. Some of these languages are still spoken today. Long before people began writing stuff down, they still had to talk to each other whether they wanted to or not, and besides, what else was there to do?

> Linguistic Note: It was through such verbal exchanges that, when they finally did get around to writing words down, the conventions of spelling began to develop. Because not everyone pronounced them the same way, there was great deviation in the way words were spelled. In fact, did you know that even as late as the turn of the seventeenth century, when Shakespeare was writing his great plays, like Hamlet, Macbeth, and Romeo and Juliet, there was no such thing as a formal dictionary? Take a look at some of that old stuff, and you will see how differently many of the words we still use today were spelled back then.

Anthropology Anyone?

Back before the Mayans, way back in the days of the Caveman, as our humanoid species was advancing slowly up that great anthropomorphic ladder (roughly 2.3 million years ago), Caveman suddenly realized that evolution had endowed him with "opposable thumbs." That is, from the shape of his hand and the splay of his fingers, Caveman realized that he could *grasp*.

This was a huge step for Caveman, and this phase of Man is known as *Homo Habilis*, a term that's used by anthropologists and that derives from *homo*, the Latin word for "Man" (as a species, not as an individual person hence the capitalization) and *habilis*, an adjective built on the verb *habere*, which means "to hold, grasp." *Homo Habilis* was "Grasping Man."

Who you calling a "Homo"?

Now, that old *Homo Habilis* grasped the fact that suddenly he could not only grasp *facts*, but also big rocks and clubs—that he could sharpen long sticks into spears—gave him an enormous advantage over other creatures in the jungle, most of which were trying to kill and eat him. Now, *he* could kill and eat *them*!

This newfound ability must have been a great comfort to him and no doubt helped him get through what must have been some lonely nights in a cold, dark cave with only his pet monkey for company! It was probably on a cold, dark, lonely night such as this that *Homo Habilis* realized he could grasp something other than spears and rocks—*his own tool!*

The fact that *Homo Habilis* had an opposable thumb led to the emergence—about a million years later—of *Homo Erectus*. What is amazing, though, is that it took *that* long for *Homo Habilis* to achieve his *Erectus!* I know this all happened way before Viagra, but c'mon...a million years is a long time to wait for anyone to get it up!

Alright, we all know that *Homo Erectus* is a term used by anthropologists that means "Standing Up Man," and not "Man With Hard-on." But I am sure that his opposable thumb helped *Homo Habilis, Homo Erectus*—as well as all the *Homos* after them—to "sharpen their spears" and "spank their monkeys" in more ways than one!

Spanking the Monkey

Masturbation, or as Woody Allen called it, "Sex with someone you love," comes from the Latin noun *manus* meaning "hand" and the verb *turbare* which means "to shake" or "to agitate." Now let's add the familiar suffix "-ion" onto the root to make it into a noun. If these three elements were spliced together, before any funky vowel shortening or consonant adding or shifting occurred, you would end up with:

manus • turba • ion

Try pronouncing that! So, two things had to happen next, both of which were meant to make the word easier to *say* (since it was already so much fun to *do!*). First, the "n" of *manus* dropped out and the root became compressed to "mas." Second, the consonant "t" was inserted into the gap between the vowel "a" of the root *turba* and the "i" of the suffix "ion." The final product became "masturbation," something we can now pronounce as easily as perform! Literally, "masturbation" is "the act of" (tion) "agitating" (*turba*) something with your hand (*manus*).

With many words, especially ones like "masturbation," people have different linguistic theories as to how they came into usage. In the case of "masturbation," some people think it may come from a combination of *manus* and the Latin verb *stuprare*, meaning "to defile," hence, the social stigma attached to it. But either way, the "hand" part remains consistent. The next time you try it you'll see it is about the only way to get the job done!

Food for Thought

Today, we find ourselves on the *Homo Sapiens* step of the anthropomorphic ladder. That means that we have risen to the point where our species is now characterized by that one thing we seem to do so infrequently—namely "thinking." Ever wonder what the next step is going to be?

You Can Do It!

We are all "able" to do many things. But if you are, for example, able to eat something, we do not say that thing is "ed*a*ble," do we? We say it is "ed*i*ble." What has changed? The "a" in "able" has changed to an "i." Now, "ible" isn't a word: "ible" is still "able," only the "a" has shortened to an "i" because "edible" is easier to say than "edable." This process is called "vowel shortening," and it happens often and somewhat predictably—generally whenever you put something in front of a root that has the letter "a" in it. When this occurs, most of the time, that "a" will change either to an "i" such as in "ible" or an "e," as we shall see below.

Fessing Up

We all know the feeling. When it's time to "fess up" you usually have to admit something to someone, to "come clean," as it were, and the hardest part about it is that you usually have to do it by *telling* them something they *don't* want to hear. More often than not this takes place face to face, in person, and can be quite unpleasant for all parties involved. We're all aware that the expression "fess up" actually contains a truncated form of the verb "to confess." The root of "fess," though, is actually *fa*, but as we have seen, its vowel changed from an "a" to an "e" once we put the "con" in front of it. A "confession" is something ("ion") spoken ("fess") in the presence of or with ("con") someone else. "Confession" is the act. "Confessor" is the person who does it, and "confessional" is the adjective meaning having the quality or characteristic ("al") of something ("ion") spoken ("fess") with someone else ("con").

"Pro"fessing

If we start fooling around with other prefixes, we will see not only this same vowel shift in play (i.e. the "a" changing to either an "e" or an "i"), but we'll also get a much clearer idea of how prevalent and important the root *fa* really is. Take, for example… me. I am a "professor." The students who encounter me every day have no idea why they call me "professor"—until, that is, they take my class! Once I get them in there, they get to cut *me* open and check out *my* ingredients.

When we break down the word, we get: *pro* + *fess* + *or*. Now, the prefix "pro" means, among other things, "in front of" or "on behalf of" and the suffix "or" is one of a group of what we call "occupational suffixes." The ending "or" usually denotes a "person who" or "thing which" does whatever the root of the word means. But what is the root of the word "professor?" As with "confessor," it is *fess*, whose root began as *fa* until we added the prefix "pro." So, a "professor" is someone who "speaks on behalf of" something, maybe even "in front of" people, or even just "about a particular thing." Unfortunately, it has nothing to do with whether or not anyone is listening!

The Professional Professor

Most people never think about the relationship between words like "professor," "profession" and even "professional." All of these words began with the root *fa*. What we have done to go from "professor" to "profession" is taken off the "occupational suffix" ("or") and replaced it with "ion," which usually indicates a noun, as in this case. So your "profession" should be something you are able to "talk about." This certainly would be considered "professional" of you!

With "professional," all we did was add the suffix "al" to the suffix "ion" to create a whole new word and even change the part of speech from a noun to an adjective. You can add more than one suffix, or prefix for that matter, to a word. But watch out, because the more you pile them up, the bigger the words get, and big words sometimes intimidate people, or—even worse—give the impression that you are trying to sound as if you know more than you probably do about something—but that's an issue we'll get to later. For now, I'll leave you with a handy piece of advice: never use "utilize" when you can use "use." And you can *always* use "use!"

Thank God It's...*Monday*?

Finally, whenever I think of the word "profession," maybe because it is based upon the root *fa*, I also think of the word "vocation," which is built on the Latin verb *vocare*, which means "to call." Although the roots *voca* and *fa* don't look anything like each other, semantically they are very similar since both have to do with speaking. A "vocation," then, is "a calling," it is something you are "called" to do. It is something special. Not everyone has one. Trust me.

We tend to blur the meaning of this word somewhat when we speak of "vocational schools" because those tend to be of the sort that train people in specific skills, often associated with "jobs" that require manual or mechanical industry, such as a computer technician, auto mechanic, dental assistant, etc. You can learn a skill so you can "get a job."

Most people who have "jobs" are different than those who have "vocations." Those with jobs are usually easy to spot. They tend to call Wednesday "Hump Day;" they're the TGIF crowd, living for the weekend.

How can you tell if you have found a "vocation" or if you just have a "job?" Easy. Just ask yourself one simple question: Am I happier Friday afternoon or Monday morning? If the answer is Friday—brother, you've got a *job*. Ever notice how someone with a "vocation" *never* needs a "vacation?"

Some Things Never Change

No one knows why, but yup, sometimes that old "a" in the root *fa* just holds its ground, even when you park a prefix in front of it. Sometimes it *does not* change. This didn't come about because those ancient Greeks and Romans were all sitting around the campfire in their togas one night deciding when that "a" would and wouldn't change. It's something that just happened over time, through the evolution of speech.

For example, the word *fanum* in Latin means *temple* or *shrine*—any sacred place where you would go to offer prayers, make vows, oaths, all those things that require "*fa*-ing," so to speak (pun intended!). But in the case of the word *fanum*, when you add the prefix "pro" onto it, the *a* stays an "a" and you get the Latin words *profanus* and *profanitas*, an adjective and a noun that come into English as "profane" and "profanity."

Profanity: Then and Now

So the idea of "profanity" arose out of a sense of religious disrespect. The logic went something like this: if you were in front of (*pro*) the shrine (*fanum*), you were not inside, among the initiated or dedicated. So you can see how it was a small step, once you add the prefix to the root for "profane" and "profanity" to take on the meaning of having contempt for what others respect. Over the centuries, the definition of "profanity" took on a broader scope to include not just words that were religiously offensive but socially offensive as well.

"Ob" Words

While we're on the topic, we might as well talk about the word "obscenity," which has nothing to do with talking at all, even though most people use it synonymously with "profanity." The word comes from the Latin verb *obscenare* which means, literally, "to sling shit." The two main elements are the prefix "ob," which means "against" or "opposite to" and often carries with it the connotation of "in your face," and the Latin noun *caenum*, which covers a whole range of shit, from mud and filth to any kind of slime in general.

> **Etymological Note:** Ever notice how most words that begin with the prefix "ob" are usually not good things? An "obstacle" just gets in your way. It "obviates" your path. If you disagree with me, you might feel an "obligation" to "object" because you think I'm being "obtuse" or trying to "obfuscate" things by making them complicated and hard to understand. You might even think I'm "obsessing" "obstreperously," that I'm "obtruding" myself and my opinions upon you. You might even wish someday to read my "obituary!"

Dipthong, the perfect gift for the lover of vowels.

The Rules of The Game

"Doing It" by *The Rules*

The ancient Greeks and Romans lived by their own particular set of societal rules—just as we do today—and believe me, a lot has changed in three thousand years! Although these rules were not written down, they were often (but not always) something entirely different than what we know of as laws. Laws didn't always exist, mind you, but there were always *The Rules*—which were important because they played such a big part in how your average ancient Greeks on the street interacted. For this reason, they also had a huge effect on their everyday language. Think about how many people you exchange words with in a day, and then compare that with how many people you actually, physically, touch!

Reach Out and Crush Someone

Today, with cell phones and e-mail, we're just throwing words out there by the billions. It's scary to realize how little we actually think about the ramifications of the words that fly out of our mouths— words that can, and often do, *affect* people. Saying the wrong word at the wrong time in the wrong place can get you killed faster than a bullet! Yes, once again we find ourselves on the dimly lit terrain of the world of the Roman *fa* and (for the Greeks) *pha*, where the tenuous relationship between the things you *say* and the things you *do* ultimately determines what happens to you in life.

Gods Who "Did" (or at Least Who Tried...)

One of the favorite pastimes of the Greek and Roman gods was to come down from their homes way up on Mt. Olympus and interfere in the lives of mortals. This usually involved, at least among the male gods, the sexual assault of (but not limited to) young girls—and our ancestors *worshiped* these people!

Now each god had his own particular way of "putting on the moves," so to speak. Zeus, for example, preferred anthropomorphism—a fancy term for changing ("morph") his shape from that of a man ("anthropo") into something else. That "something" else usually turned out to be an animal of some kind—usually the cute kind—cuddly and furry and sure to attract the attention of, and be irresistible to, a young, unsuspecting girl.

Hail to the *Chief*?

A typical outing for Zeus would go something like this: he'd come down to earth in the form of, say, a little kitty cat, and lure some poor girl off into the woods, and then—SHAZAM!—suddenly change back to the huge, mighty brute of a god that he was and take what he understood to be, as Philip Roth put it so well, the "phallic entitlement" that went with being the King of the Gods.

This was how the ancient Greeks and Romans viewed their world as dominated by the mythologically empowered polytheism that they created for themselves. The raping of young girls (and sometimes boys) by the gods was part of their society. This was part of *The Rules*, and if the girl refused, it was *she* who was not playing by them. If she were to deny a god the enjoyment of exercising his—Roth again—"sexual rapacity," then she would pay a stiff penalty—one that would be even *stiffer* than the one she had just refused!

This was how Zeus, the god they respected and worshipped the most, got his kicks! And on top of it all, Zeus was *married!* To a goddess named Hera. And Hera knew damn well what old Zeus was up to with all his "catting around," so they fought all the time. You could say it was a somewhat dysfunctional relationship. And on top of it all, Hera was not only Zeus' *wife*, she was also his *sister*. I guess they really wanted to keep the money in the family!

A Girl Who "Didn't" (or Tried Not To...)

Another god who shared this kind of leisure activity was Apollo. But Apollo didn't waste his time with all that anthropo*whatever* stuff. His attitude was that "Earth girls were easy," and so he tried to smooth-talk his way into the old "poontang." Well, one day, Apollo comes down from high Olympus, riding his sun-powered chariot convertible (with leather interior) and spots a young girl by the name of Cassandra, picking daisies in the middle of a beautiful meadow. So Apollo, he turns on the old charm, and asks Cassandra if she'd like to go for a little ride in his "love buggy."

Now, Cassandra also knows *The Rules*. She understands what he's after, but she's spunky and tries to bargain with Apollo. She'll give it up, she says, but only if he gives her a present first. Apollo accepts, saying "Okay sugarpop, if you'll just hop on in here with me, I'll give you a special gift—the kind of gift only a god can give."

And what does that turn out to be? Flowers? Diamond earrings in a bright blue Tiffany box? Hardly. In return for a little of the old "in-out," for a shot at getting to do the "horizontal hoola," for a chance to "make the beast with two backs" or "do the dance that has no steps" with Cassandra, Apollo gives her the gift of *prophecy*.

 Etymological Note: By now, you should be able to recognize the root pha when you see it, even when it is in disguise as it is here. If we break down "prophecy," we get (pro • phe • cy). If we apply our rule of vowel shortening, the root phe started out as pha, until the addition of the prefix "pro" caused it to change from an "a" to an "e." So what did Apollo give Cassandra? The ability to tell (pha) the future before ("pro") it happens.

Tease Me, Tease Me…

Cassandra takes the deal—what choice has she, really? Apollo's going to have her one way or the other, so why not get a little something for herself in the bargain? Now, according to *The Rules*, once a god gives you a gift, he can't take it back. So when Apollo steps down from the chariot to take her away, Cassandra, believing she can outwit this god, tells him "Not so fast." She wants to go home first, freshen-up, maybe do her hair, change her *peplos*, put on some make-up—all that "chick stuff." Apollo falls for it, and they agree to meet back in the meadow in a couple of hours, say, around sixish?

…Just Don't *Leave* Me!

Well, sixish rolls around and there's Apollo waiting in his chariot. And waiting… And then he finally gets it: Cassandra's a no-show! He, Apollo, a *god*, has been "stood up" by a mortal girl! She's broken *The Rules*—she didn't *do* what she *said* she'd do! What's more, she got the gift of prophecy from him without letting him "bury the bone," or "hide the sausage," or "lay some pipe," or "spear the hairy doughnut," or even "do it doggy style," or "thrust the pink chariot up the back street" and "ride the Hershey Highway." She got away without having to "get boned," or "grab her ankles," or "dance on the ceiling," or "play hide the spring roll," or "ride the baloney pony." She must have realized that she'd probably also have to "give him a hummer," or "polish his helmet," or "gobble the goose," or "smoke the big one," or "play the meat flute," or "take a lip lock on his fudgesicle" for a while first. And even after all that, she probably wouldn't even reach the "Big O," or get to "ring her bell," or "blow her juice." But, of course, Apollo, he's certainly going to get to "shoot *his* wad," and "blow *his* load," and probably want to do it on her face (with heavy eye contact) or on her tits, or, knowing Apollo, both. And frankly, thought Cassandra—*fuck* that!

You have to hand it to her. Clever girl. A real "ballbuster." Cassandra the "cocktease," as she was known from then on. But there was one thing she forgot. Apollo may not have been able to take back his gift, but you don't go around giving a god a case of the "blue balls," you don't get him all "freaky" and "horny" and leave him, frankly, "fuckstrated" and think you're going to get away with it! Maybe Apollo couldn't take the gift of prophecy back, but there wasn't anything stopping him from giving her another gift—this time more of a curse, really—and that was that even though she could now tell the future, whenever she tried to share her visions, no one would ever believe her.

> **Mythological Note:** "Horny" is a word that most people use without understanding where it comes from. There is a very good chance (I say "chance" because how can you *prove* something like this?) that "horny" is an allusion to the Egyptian god, Amon. Amon was the male god of fertility, and Isis was the Egyptian goddess of fertility. The two were lovers. So, if your job is to satisfy the goddess of fertility, you'd better be a walking "love machine," a round-the-clock "hoseman" twenty-four/seven, or you're going to find yourself out of a job, pal. Now, whenever the gods are depicted in ancient art, they are generally shown holding or wearing something that uniquely identified them—so the viewer could know whom he was looking at. Athena was always accompanied by the owl; Zeus is often shown wielding his trademark thunderbolt; Apollo had his bow and quiver full of arrows—well, Amon is always depicted with horns coming out of his head. So, if you're "horny," you're acting like Amon, who literally always was!

Daphne

Cassandra wasn't the only girl who jilted Apollo. When he tried to seduce Daphne, a woodland nymph and daughter of the river god Peneius, she took off running through the woods to escape him. When he finally caught up with her, she had reached the banks of her father, the river Peneius. So she prayed to her father to save her from having to "give it up" for this sex-crazed god. Peneius granted his daughter's prayer, and just as Apollo laid his hands on her, her feet took root on the river bank, her skin turned into hard bark and from the tips of her fingers sprouted the leaves of a Laurel tree.

Apollo may have been disappointed again, but he tried to be a good sport about it After all, what choice had he? So in honor of Daphne, he decorated his lyre with leaves and sprigs of laurel that he plucked from the branches of her tree. Deep down, Apollo thought of himself as a nice guy. But he was learning that not only do nice guys finish last, a lot of the time, nice guys don't even get started!

 Art Historical Note: The *Galleria Borghese* in Rome houses one of the world's most famous collections of Baroque art. Of the entire collection, it is Gian Lorenzo Bernini's *Apollo and Daphne* that is considered the supreme treasure of the museum. In the life-size marble sculpture, Bernini's genius moved him to catch the very moment when Daphne begins her transformation into a Laurel tree at the precise moment Apollo lays his hands on her.

The Sibyl of Cumae

Having been shot down twice, Apollo really needed to "get some" and he needed it *badly*. So he next tried to put the moves on the Sibyl of a place called Cumae, a cave by a lake in southern Italy. This time he tried the old Cassandra tactic again: he grants the Sibyl a gift. Not prophecy this time—look how *that* had turned out! No, this time Apollo grants the Sibyl the gift of a long life. She could live "for as many years as grains of sand she could hold in her hands." Say what you want about Apollo, but when he wanted some snatch, he *could* get pretty creative with his gifts! But this time, the Sibyl of Cumae borrowed a page out of Cassandra's playbook and once she had picked up the sand, looking greedily down at the golden pile in her hands, said she'd changed her mind! Sorry…

Once again, according to *The Rules*, Apollo could not take back the gift, but he could give her another one. And boy did he ever! The Sibyl may have bargained for an extra year of life for each grain of sand she held in her hands (and Sibyls were known for having large hands) only now for each year she lived, she would age *ten*!

Marpessa

Then there was Marpessa, a mortal girl whom Zeus gave to Apollo in order to assuage the god after Marpessa's husband, Idas, defeated Apollo in a chariot race. Now you don't beat Apollo in *anything*, let alone a chariot race! But when Marpessa chose her mortal husband over Apollo, and begged Zeus to honor her wish, Apollo was so insulted to be passed over by a mortal that he just slunk off in shame, blue balls and all. It was, after all, Zeus who had set up the whole competition and who in the end honored Marpessa's wish to remain faithful to her husband. And even Apollo knew, you *do not fuck* with Zeus!

Sinope

When Apollo first caught sight of Sinope, he was a goner. Sooooo beautiful! Sooooo young! And on top of it all, a *virgin*—which were becoming harder and harder to find these days! This time, Apollo was sure his luck was going to change. But like Cassandra and the Sibyl, Sinope also knew *The Rules*. "Here we go again," thought Apollo, "another fucking gift! Who do they think I am, Santa Fucking Clause?" But Sinope—known to be a bit of a "player" herself—she seemed to be enjoying herself. Sure, she'd roll over, but only if he granted her— "Don't tell me," said Apollo, wearily, "a *gift*, right?"

Wrong! Sinope doesn't want a gift. No, what she wants is a fucking *wish*. And while Apollo is trying to figure out what the *fucking difference* is between the one and the other, Sinope adds that it has to be a "secret" wish. Sounds harmless enough—and because by this point Apollo is probably "hotter than a fresh-fucked fox in a forest fire," he'd be willing to give *anyone anything* just to get into *someone's peplos*! So he grants her her "secret wish" only to find out, as he's climbing out of his armor, that Sinope's secret wish—which he already went ahead and granted her—was to remain a virgin for the rest of her life! He...*just...can...not...win*!

Hyacinthus

At this point, Apollo was so desperate he started hitting on young boys. Things were actually looking good with one of them, a boy by the name of Hyacinthus. Now, Hyacinthus might have only been about twelve or fourteen, but he was not about to let Apollo "pack his fudge" for a handful of sand! After all, he'd been down the "Hershey Highway" once before with a man by the name of Thamyris (who is said, incidentally, to have been the world's first homosexual), and he knows that old back door access is worth holding out for!

Hyacinthus was also the son of Amyclas, the king of Sparta. Now those Spartans were into sports. Big time. Hyacinthus, being just a kid, wants to play a little discus with Apollo first. He wants to be the first kid on his block to say he played discuss with a god! So Apollo humors the kid, and they start to play. Hyacinthus throws the discus at Apollo, and Apollo is supposed to pick it up and throw it back (think Frisbee ancient Greek style). But when Apollo does, he forgets just how powerful he is—what with being a god and all—and when he lets that discus fly it just comes soaring at little Hyacinthus with such velocity that it takes his head clean off. The poor kid probably never even saw it coming!

> **Horticultural Note:** They say it was from the blood of Hyacinthus' severed head that the flower that bears his name first sprung.

Cyparissus

This was just not Apollo's day. At this rate, he couldn't get his dick wet with bucket and a garden hose! He's still determined to try one more time. So, he drops in on Cyparissus, the son of Telephus, a beautiful boy from the island of Ceos for whom Apollo had had the hotsy-totsies for a long time. But, like all his other relationships, this one was doomed to fail before it could even begin.

There was this sacred stag, said to have been tamed by the nymphs of Carrhea, and it was Cyparissus' favorite pet. Everywhere that Cyparissus went, the deer was sure to follow. He would spend hours with it, grazing with it in the fields, grooming its beautiful auburn coat. So, Apollo knows he's going to have to hang out with the damned deer, at least until he can figure out some way to lure the boy away from the fucking thing. So, the three of them go out to have a picnic under the shade of a sprawling oak tree. As the afternoon wore on, the stag started to get sleepy and laid down to take a nap! Apollo figures this is his chance…

So Apollo tries to snuggle up to Cyparissus. That failing, he even tries wooing the boy with a few slow tunes on his lyre, but Cyparissus was not quite in the mood just yet and felt like he wanted to do a little *hunting* first! For *Chrissakes*! Didn't anyone like to just plain *fuck* anymore? Now, Cyparissus wants Apollo to show him how to hold his spear. And not his "spear," but his actual *spear*! "I'll show you how to hold your spear, all right," thought Apollo, but there seems to be no getting around the fact that the little bastard *still* wants to do a some hunting first. Well, at least that goddamned stag was out of the way!

So while the stag snoozed under the tree, off they went into the bush. In no time, they spotted a wild boar muscling through the bush. Apollo showed Cyparissus how to cock the spear behind his ear and take aim. "Go for it!" whispers Apollo, so Cyparissus lets the spear fly. At the last moment, the boar spooked and took off into the woods. The spear sailed on through the trees and slammed into the side of Cyparissus' beloved, sleeping stag. *Oooops*!

So heartbroken was the young man that he asks Apollo to grant him the gift of being able to go on mourning and weeping for the rest of his life. Apollo grants the wish—what else *can* he do?—and suddenly the kid starts bawling his eyes out. *Great*. Mourning the death of your favorite pet doesn't exactly put you in the mood to suck dick, let alone take it up the ass. But on top of it all, and I don't think anyone saw this coming, Cyparissus cried so much that in no time he had wept himself dry. Literally. Faster than you could say "beef jerky" the boy just shriveled up and died right then and there! It was the first recorded case of "Death by Desiccation." In honor of the boy, Apollo turned him into a tree and named it the Cypress after him. It seemed to be his day for naming trees.

Is It "In" Yet?

Just as societies have rules, so do their languages. In Chapter One, we briefly touched on the various ways to negate a root by adding a "negatory prefix" onto it. In this chapter, we'll look more closely at how to negate words using both Latin and Greek prefixes.

In Latin, a prefix can have different meanings depending on the root to which it gets attached and the context in which the word is used. But it's not all that hard to get a handle on them, as most prefixes have to do with either direction (up/down; in/out; before/after, etc.) or negation. The prefix "in" is one that has to do with both.

As far as direction is concerned, it pretty much means in English what it means in Latin: with verbs of motion (e.g., move, throw, run, etc.), "in" means "into" as in, "He drove the chariot *into* the garage" or "Achilles thrust his sword *into* Hector." With static verbs, like the verb "to be," the prefix "in" indicates a place where something or someone "is," such as: "The chariot is *in* the garage" or "Paris is *in* bed giving Helen the high hard one." When "in" isn't being used in these two ways, it usually negates the root, such as in the words "inaccurate" or "individual." Another way to negate is with "un," a variant of "in" that changed due to centuries of travel throughout Europe. Examples using this prefix are also numerous in our language, for example: The Trojan War was "unavoidable."

When Consonants Collide...

In the previous chapter, we saw how vowels can change when you start compounding words. We saw, particularly, how the vowel "a" in the root of a word will change either to an "i" or an "e" when you add a prefix onto it. In this chapter, we'll look at what happens with consonants, particularly when a prefix that ends in a consonant collides with a root that begins with one.

As we saw in Chapter One, with the word "impotency," the rule is that when the "n" in the prefix "in" gets parked up next to a word that begins with a consonant, the "n" usually changes ("in" + "potency" = "impotency").

Seeing as we've been talking about rules and laws and such, if we take the root *leg*, from the Latin noun *lex*, meaning "law,, and negate it, we would add the prefix "in." What we end up with, however, is not "inlegal," but "illegal." In general, the rule is that whenever you put any prefix that ends with a consonant in front of a root that begins with one, you drop the consonant on the end of the prefix and double the one that begins the root.

"Illegal" is also another fine example of how words in English can be broken down into the same familiar template (prefix + root + suffix). In this case, "illegal" is an adjective meaning something that has the quality or characteristic ("al") of being against ("in") the law ("leg").

The same thing happens even when we're not negating something. For example, the Latin verb *portare* means "to carry." The root is *port*. Now, if we're going to carry something from underneath, we'd use the prefix "sub." But when we splice them together, we don't end up with "subport," we get "support." There's our rule in play again! We drop the last consonant of the prefix and double the first consonant of the root. It all goes back to making words easier to say.

... Accidents Can Happen

Whenever you see a word that has a doubling of consonants up near the front, like "support," or "illegal," you are probably on a literary collision site. An accident has happened. In fact, the word "accident" is an excellent example not only of the rules we've been discussing in this chapter regarding consonants, but also of the rules governing "vowel shortening" that we observed in the previous chapter.

If we climb in and pull apart the wreckage of the "accident" we get: (*ac • cid • ent.*) First things first, let's look at the prefix. Now, "ac" is *not* a prefix in Latin. The original prefix was "ad" and means "toward" or "upon." When the "d" of "ad" collided with the "c" of the root, the "d" dropped off and we doubled the "c." Now let's examine the root to see what vowel changes occurred.

The root "cid" derives from the Latin verb *cadere*, which means to fall. So, the original root was *cad* until it collided with the prefix "ad," and the "a" shortened to an "i" (*cid* = *cad*). So an "accident" is something that "falls" (*cad*) "upon" ("ad") someone.

 Free legal advice: This rule about dropping the last consonant of the prefix and doubling the first one of the root, like all rules, has its exceptions. Take, for example, the word "subpoena." It is easy to see that it is made up of the prefix "sub" meaning "under" and *poena* which is the Latin word for "punishment." But here, unlike with "support," the "b" hangs in there. The word *subpoena* refers to a legal instrument that forces you to show up in court. So if you get *"subpoenaed,"* you had better show up, because if you don't, you are under ("sub") threat of punishment (*poena*).

Science Geek...Er, Greek

Whenever scientists discover stuff, they always go either to the Latin or the Greek language to come up with a name for it. Why is this? Neither language has been spoken for thousands of years, and even when they were, they were never spoken *here*! Well, it's not that they're showing off, or because they want whatever it is that they've discovered, or invented, or maybe even re-invented, to sound important. Nor is it that they're just trying to make it hard on regular folks like us.

The real reason is that until fairly recently, (and by "fairly recently" I'm talking about, say, the turn of the twentieth century), anyone who was well educated had at some point learned their Latin and Greek. So a scientist working in Poland and one working in China could both communicate through these two ancient tongues. Today, everybody just learns English, but the tradition has stuck around—scientists still go back to ancient Greek and Latin to name their stuff.

I always imagine that many big corporations—particularly those that produce chemical or pharmaceutical products—have some geek like me tucked away in the basement who knows his Latin and Greek roots and upon whom they can call, when they've invented something new, to come up with a fancy name for it. And he must be one busy guy, let me tell you, as today we have over seven million names for all the different chemical compounds we've invented—with no sign of slowing down!

There is also a certain elegance, you'll find, in going back to the Greek and Latin languages when trying to name scientific stuff particularly when it takes you down the road of Greek and Roman mythology, for which there has always been a fascination the world over. For example, I recently read about a scientist who wanted to combine human embryonic cells with cells from the embryo of a monkey, ape, or other animal to create a kind of hybrid out of the two. When he went to patent this idea, he had to come up with a name for this creature. Since his name wasn't Baron Von Frankenstein, he had to come up with something original. So where did he go?

You guessed it! Into the tomes of Greek and Roman mythology he dove, and when he emerged he had his name, he was going to call his creation the "Chimaera." Not a wise move, when you consider that the Chimaera was a fire-breathing she-monster with the head and forefeet of a lion, the body and hind quarters of a goat and the tail of a serpent. The Chimaera terrorized Greece until Bellerophon, with the aid of the winged-horse Pegasus, killed her by showering her with arrows from the air. The patent was turned down (thank god!), because that's the last thing we need running around loose on the planet!

What Happens When You Don't

Maybe the reason scientists persist in going back to Greek and Latin vocabulary and mythology is that when you don't, you can end up with some silly sounding stuff. For instance, there was another scientist working along the same lines, using a similar methodology. This guy was combining the cells of a sheep and a goat. But when it came time to file for the patent, he didn't go back to the ancient Greeks to name his creature. The name he came up with was "Geep." That's right, "Geep"— i.e. part goat, (that's the "g" part), and part sheep (that's that "eep" part). Now I don't know about you, but as horrible a creature as the Chimaera was, "Geep" (and it's a hard "g" by the way) just sounds plain stupid!

We don't even have to get into gene splicing to see other examples of how scientists continue to go back to these ancient languages to name stuff. Just take a stroll through your friendly neighborhood pharmacy and you'll see what I mean. It's all around us. It's no coincidence that the popular facial cream women apply at night is called *Noxema* once you know that the Latin word for night is *nox*. The elderly take *Geritol* without knowing that its name derives from the Greek word *geron* meaning old man. The next time you come down with a cough, try *Robotussin*. It ought to work, as *tussis* is the Latin word for cough!

Saying No in Greek

As we saw briefly in Chapter One, to negate a root that comes into English from Greek, we don't use the Latin prefix "in." Instead, we use that little letter that does so much: what linguists call the "alpha privative," because it "deprives" the root of its meaning, as in "Paris' abduction of Helen was *a*moral."

May I Cut In?

Yes you may, but you might be sorry if you do! Why is that? Because someone already did, and we all saw what happened, and we've been trying like crazy not to let it happen ever again! The Greek root *tom* means "to cut." Now, if we want to negate that root, it's easy. We just stick the "alpha privative" onto the front of it, and we've got a word for something that cannot be cut, namely: the "atom."

At the time scientists discovered it, they thought that it was the smallest particle of matter in the universe, that it was unable to be cut. So they called down to their Greek Geek in the basement and described it to him and said they needed a name for it. So he consulted his Greek lexicon and came up with "atom."

Bugging Out

Had our Greek Geek gone to his Latin dictionary instead of his Greek lexicon, he might have chosen the verb *sectare*, which also means "to cut" and whose root is *sect*. Then, following the rules of Latin negation, he would have added the prefix "in" onto the front of the root *sect* and come up with "insect." Uh-oh! For obvious reasons—foremost among them that it was already taken, he couldn't have used it. Why?

Because in the word "insect," the prefix "in" does not negate, it just means "in." An "insect" is so named because when people first started studying bugs, they noticed that most of them had segmented bodies. They were made up of "sections." The word "insect" is simply the Latin translation of the Greek word *entomos* (εντομος), which also means something that is "cut up into" pieces. It *is* from the Greek word for "bug," by the way, that we get the term "entomologist" for a person who studies them. But it would have sounded pretty silly had we named the atomic bomb an "insect!"

When Atoms Collide

Even though we now know that the atom *can*, in fact, be cut, no one is about to rename it. But, they should. Because when you split an atom, its particles fly off and collide with other atoms causing a chain reaction that releases a huge amount of energy really quickly that you don't want to get in the way of. The first Atomic Bomb was made in 1945 by J. Robert Oppenheimer and the Manhattan Project team. And they've been making them ever since—not Openheimer, just everybody else! But if you think about it, you'll realize that the term "atomic energy," or "atomic power" is, in fact, an "oxymoron." But we'll tackle those in Chapter Eight.

 Historical Note: It is reported that Oppenheimer's brother, after watching the detonation of the first atomic bomb at the testing site at Los Alamos on 16 July, 1945, quoted a verse out of the Hindu scripture *Bhagavad Gita*: "I am become death, the destroyer of worlds." As for Oppenheimer himself, no one recorded his exact words, but they were probably something like: "Holy Fuck—it *worked!*"

When Alphas Collide

When you want to negate a root in Greek using the "alpha privative," and that root begins with a consonant, like *tom* did above, you're fine. But when the root begins with a vowel, you have to insert the consonant "n" between them so you can pronounce the damn thing. That's where we get our convention of adding the letter "n" to the indefinite article "a" when we say "a book," but "an apple," remember?

Stopping the Pain!

Nobody likes to be in pain. When you have a headache, you might take an *analgesic* like aspirin. The word *analgesic* is simply made up of the Greek root *alg* (αλγ) with the alpha privative on the front of it. Since the root begins with a vowel, we added the *n* onto it. The alpha privative is very common in our language, so we will keep our eyes out for more words that have it.

 Etymological note: Even though it may have caused you a lot of pain in high school, the word "Algebra" does not come from the ancient Greek root *alg*, as is the case with "analgesic." It's actually an Arabic word (*al-jabr*) and means, literally, "the reduction." This makes sense, because Algebra sure went a long way toward the reduction of my GPA in high school!

School Words

Paging...Doctor Cerutti

On the first day of class each semester, I write my name on the blackboard and inform my students that they may call me—at least to my face—"Steve," or if they are uncomfortable with that, they may call me, "Mr. Cerutti." But I warn them that whenever someone addresses me as "Mr. Cerutti" I always feel like my father. If they want to call me "Dr. Cerutti," that's fine too, but then I always feel like the son my father never had. Why? Because we associate the title of "Doctor" with the medical profession.

When I ask my class why they call their professors "Doctor," several students usually say it is because we have a Ph.D. Well, what does *that* mean? Pause. A hand goes up. Because the letters stand for "Doctor of Philosophy?" *Correct!* So, what does *that* mean? If your philosophy gets sick, I can cure it?

Degrees of Distinction

The title "Doctor of Philosophy" is a hybrid—a combination of both Latin and Greek words and their roots. The word "doctor" is made up of the Latin root *doct,* from the Latin verb *docere,* which means "to teach," plus the "occupational suffix" "or" meaning "one who" does whatever the root means. "Philosophy" is a combination of the Greek root *phil* (φιλ), which means "to like" or "to love" (and is most often encountered as the suffix "phile" meaning "lover of" whatever the root of the word means, plus the Greek root *soph* (σοφ), which means "wisdom" or "knowledge." So someone with a Ph.D. is, literally, "someone who is going to teach you to love learning for learning's sake." *Good luck!*

Historical Note: The Greek term for "professor" was "sophist," based, obviously, on the Greek root *soph* (σοφ). Sophists were known to travel from town to town teaching skills in order to help people earn a better living. The subjects they taught, the methodology they used, and the level of their competence varied greatly. Some were highly respected and sought after, while others had the reputation of being quacks who covered up their ignorance by being deliberately provocative. Perhaps the fact that they offered their services free of charge—although tipping *was* allowed, if not outright *encouraged*—enabled them to pursue this line of work!

Philosophy 101

Although some people consider it simply "mental masturbation," the word "philosophy" means, literally, learning and thinking about stuff just because you like to. In the initials of the Ph.D., we abbreviate the first letter of the word "philosophy" as "Ph" and not just as "P," because "Ph" is the correct transliteration of the sound produced by the Greek letter "φ" (say: "fee"), which is the first letter in the Greek word φιλοσοφια.

So, how did the word "doctor," which has nothing to do with medicine, get all tangled up in the medical profession? In Medieval Latin, a *doctor* was a religious teacher. Later, in the fourteenth century, it had come to mean anyone who held the highest degree from a university, and the "Doctor of Medicine" was the earliest such recorded degree. Today, the Ph.D. outranks the M.D. as the highest degree a university can bestow. But the medical connotation just kind of hung around as the term crossed the Atlantic and arrived in this country in 1712.

Today, most medical centers are connected with universities and refer to themselves as "teaching hospitals." In fact, it is from the medical profession that we get the phrase "watch one, do one, teach one" when referring to "The Three Basic Steps of Learning." The original phrase was "medical doctor" because part of your responsibility was to "teach one." Then the "medical" just dropped off.

The Three Basic Steps of Learning

The "Three Basic Steps of Learning" is a concept that dates back to the very earliest days of ancient Rome and was associated primarily with the duties of the Vestal Virgins. The Vestal Virgins were a religious cult that required a thirty year commitment on the part of the initiant and whose most important responsibility, among the many that were imposed upon her, was to keep the eternal fire of Rome burning in the Temple of Vesta. In Chapter Two, we saw how much pressure was placed on girls to produce male children at a very young age and the lamentable consequences that awaited the poor girl who was unable to do so. But marriage wasn't the only option a father had when deciding his daughter's future. There was another way to go.

The grim facts were these: if you were the father of a young daughter in ancient Rome, you had two options. Option #1: arrange a marriage that would be politically beneficial to your family and hope your daughter produced sons. Option #2: find some way to get her accepted into the cult of the Vestal Virgins.

The Vestal Virgins

The cult of the Vestal Virgins was one of the oldest, most sacrosanct, revered branches of the state religion, dating back to 715 B.C.—nearly to the founding of Rome itself. So if as a father, you got your little Chastity accepted into the cult, then you would be relived from all the worries that went with having to marry her off. Not only would it mean a huge boost for the social status of your family, but being a member of this group of priestesses also gave your daughter an immense power not enjoyed by other women. As a Vestal Virgin, she was part of an important link between the state and the gods. It was a huge responsibility, but the job also came with its own set of perks!

The Vestal Virgins got their own bodyguards; whenever they went out into the streets of Rome, they traveled by private limo; and they had the power to pardon condemned criminals. But the biggest perk of all? Whenever the Vestals attended the games in the Circus Maximus or the Colosseum, they always got the best seats in the house—in The Emperor's private box—front row and center, right on the fifty-yard line!

Giving up "Giving It Up"

Upon becoming a Vestal Virgin, the young girl took a mandatory vow of celibacy for the next thirty years of her life. But it didn't end there. They didn't get all these perks just for agreeing "not to give it up" until they were forty! Being a Vestal Virgin meant you had perform important duties and shoulder great responsibilities. It fell upon you to perform specific rites essential to the running of the state religion, and many of these duties were often physically demanding, and sometimes could be dangerous. For these reasons, in order even to be considered, the girl had to be between the ages of six and ten years old, had to have certain physical qualities (among them beauty, but also health and strength). They were also required to have free-born Roman parents, both of whom were living.

Watch One, Do One, Teach One

If she made the grade, the girl would be legally separated from her parents and moved into the House of the Vestals in the Roman Forum. This would be her home for the next thirty years, during which time she spent the first ten years learning the duties of a Vestal; the second ten performing them; and the third ten teaching them to the next generation of Vestal wannabees.

The duties of the Vestals included, mainly, keeping the eternal fire of Vesta burning in the Temple of Vesta, which was right there in the Forum (and still is today). Vestals also had to haul water from sacred springs, some of them miles away, to purify the house of the Vestals as well as the temple itself, which was a separate structure, though connected to the house. They had to bake sacrificial cakes to be used in religious ceremonies. The House of the Vestals also served as the depository for public documents such as wills, credit records, etc., and they had to keep track of all of these.

Failure to perform her duties—or even to perform them well—was a real no-no. If, for instance, one of the Vestals let the fire of Vesta go out, she was dragged into a dark room, stripped naked, and whipped! This was usually overseen by the high priest of Rome, the Pontifex Maximus. For many years, Julius Caesar held the position of Pontifex Maximus. We'll talk more about this character a little later on.

Life after Vestal Virgining

Once your service as a Vestal Virgin was up, then *what?* After thirty years, a Vestal Virgin was free, should she so choose, to re-enter society and perhaps even marry. But—because there wasn't that big of a market for forty-year old virgins on the Roman singles circuit—she could choose simply to stay on and continue her service to Vesta. And it seems that that's what most of them ended up doing.

But Remember...*No* Hanky-Panky

Staying on as a Vestal Virgin, however, still meant sticking to your vow of celibacy. If a Vestal Virgin ever strayed from the path of the straight and narrow—if she decided one day that the "do one" part of The Three Basic Steps of Learning suddenly meant something of a more carnal nature—the punishment was swift and severe. The girl was carried through the Forum in a covered litter to a place called the *Campus Sceleratus,* which translates, roughly, into "Field of Torment" or "Wickedness" and it lay just outside the Colline Gate on the north side of the city.

What awaited her there was not going to be pleasant. She would be placed in an underground chamber that contained a narrow cot, an oil lamp, and a small amount of bread and water. They would seal the chamber, leaving her to die either from starvation or asphyxiation. A guard would be posted to make sure no escape or rescue was attempted. After a certain period of time, the body would be removed and carried to the Forum where it was be burned on a pyre under the auspices of state funerary rites and customs.

As for the poor guy with whom she "did it," a much different, and even more bizarre fate awaited. First, they would beat the snot out of him in the Forum, then cut off his nose and stitch him up in a canvas sack along with a snake, a dog, and a monkey. Finally, they would throw the sack into the Tiber River. It's safe to say that not that many Vestal Virgins were tempted to stray from their vows. And if one of them did start to feel a little spunky, she probably had a hard time finding any takers.

What Leisure Time?

My students are always shocked when they learn that the root of the word "school" comes from the Greek root *schol* (σχολ), which means "leisure time." Showing up for 8 AM classes, reading the books, doing the homework, writing the papers, taking the tests normally just means a lot of *work*, right?

Wrong! We think this way because for us in modern society—certainly in America—school is something you *have* to do. In fact, it's the *law*. Most of my students view college as just "more school" that they *have* to go on and do like they *had* to go to high school, the only difference being that in college they can smoke and drink and sleep with each other a lot easier. It's hard for them to imagine a time when this was not always the case—when "public" schools and state university systems didn't exist. When there was no such thing as a student loan!

Education Roman Style

Back in the days of Julius Caesar, there was no such law requiring children to attend formal schooling. Only a very small percentage of the population actually had access to any formal education whatsoever. You had to know Latin in order to get into the Roman army, okay, and that was considered a lifetime career at the end of which was a healthy pension (if you made it!).

But beyond the acquisition of rudimentary skills like learning your Latin, you were pretty much on your own and would be expected to work the family farm or business from the youngest age at which you were able. Who cared about studying history, reading poetry or learning to play the lyre when there were fields to plow and cows to milk?

A formal education was not easy to get. If a father had the money, he would send his son away from home to receive his education at a private school—the best schools being in Athens, Greece (very expensive); or he could hire a private tutor to come to the house (very, *very* expensive). Most working families didn't have the kind of money to do either, so most sons grew up learning the family business and eventually taking it over. Now if the family business began to make money and the father started setting aside a few *sentences*, and his son after him did the same, and likewise his son after him—then maybe, *just maybe*, the family would have saved up enough money in two (or three) generations to be able to afford to send perhaps *one* of its great, great, great grandsons to a school in Athens.

The root *schol* is also where we get the words "scholar" and "scholarship." When we think of a "scholar" most people picture someone spending long hours pondering great ideas, writing down his thoughts, even publishing them. You find scholars in libraries doing their "scholarship." Can you see how the idea of "free" or "leisure" time is associated with this type of lifestyle and activity? It's simple, really. A scholar of ancient Rome, say, can sit around writing a book about *The Toilets of Pompeii* because he's not out fixing them all day long!

A scholar's work is his "scholarship," but the word also applies to the money some students receive to help them pay for their education. It buys them the free time to attend class. Without a scholarship, they would have to go out and get a job and work to raise the money to pay for the free time to go to class.

> **Historical Note:** Back before there were such study aids as *Cliff's Notes*—academic guidebooks to help students better understand great literary works—there were people whose job it was to annotate such works. Seeing as this was also before the printing press, when books had to be copied by hand, these notes had to be hand-written in the margins of the texts. You can imagine how time-consuming a job this must have been. The people who had the knowledge—and, more importantly, the *leisure time*—to do this were called "scholiasts" and the notes they jotted down in the margins of people's books were called *scholia*.

Step One: Matriculation

If you happen to be one of the lucky ones who can get the money to buy the leisure time to go to school—particularly college—you have to "matriculate," that is, register for classes, pay your fees, etc. "Matriculation" is a big, fancy word that simply comes from the Latin word *mater*, where we get our word "mother." In earlier Latin, it can also mean "womb," so the word "matriculation," is actually a nice metaphor for entering the protective walls of the university, what will someday be your *Alma Mater*!

Head of the Class!

What does it mean to be a good student? Well, a good place to start would be to answer the question What does the word "student" actually mean? Because education was far out of most people's financial reach, only wealthy, free-born Roman citizens got a chance to have one; therefore, because so few people got one, *everyone* wanted one.

The root of the word "student" is *stude* and comes from the Latin verb *studere*, which means "to be eager." As a result, the word "student" literally means "one who is eager," and it means what it means not because that's what we teachers expect, or hope our students will be (which, so often, they are not), but because in the ancient days of Rome, you had to be really, really eager to get an education. We have seen how generations of a single family would work and toil and save their *sesterces* and *denarii's* so that a single grandchild, perhaps, might one day get to go to school. This was the only way to raise the family name out of the lower classes.

> **Historical Note:** Although the value of currency fluctuated wildly over the many centuries of Roman rule throughout the Mediterranean world, a *sestertius* was a relatively common copper coin, whereas the Roman *denarius* was made of silver and was equal to about a day's wages for a Roman soldier, depending, of course, upon rank, etc.

Social Climbing

The word "education" is made up of three elements, once again our familiar template: *e • duc • ation*. Now the root of this word, *duc*, comes from the Latin verb *ducere* which means to lead. The word also contains the prefix "e" (a variant of "ex") and means "out of."

 So, literally, the word "education" means the "act of leading one out" of something. Out of *what*? In ancient Rome, it was out of the poverty of the lower classes and into the wealth of the upper classes because it was only through the formal education of, say, one's son, that a family could move up socially. With an education, that son could go on to a career in politics and thereby marry into a better family, have better children who would go to better schools, marry into better families, eventually get into politics and gain real power and influence.

This was how most of the important families in ancient Rome got to *be* important families. The same is also true today. Our forty-second president, William Jefferson Clinton, was born in a coldwater cabin in a shithole called Hope, Arkansas and raised by a single mother. Yet, through hard work, sacrifice, and "education" he became a Rhodes Scholar and went on to become the leader of the free world—whether he "inhaled" or not! There are other examples on both sides of "the aisle," but the point is, whatever your politics, very few people have ever risen that high in the world without the benefit of a formal education!

Historical Note: It is from the fact that an education was only available to free-born Roman citizens that we get the term "Liberal Arts." The Latin adjective *liber* means "free." In ancient Rome, there were the *Artes Liberales*, or the subjects that a well-to-do free-born man would be expected to learn. The original *Artes Liberales* were: mathematics; geometry; music; astronomy; grammar; rhetoric; and dialectics—a fancy term for knowing how to win an argument. Then there were the *Artes Serviles* ("servile skills") which were the manual chores that a slave had to learn to serve his master as he was told. These covered anything from cooking or serving a meal, to shoveling horseshit. There was a light at the end of the tunnel of servitude, however, and that was that it was often customary for slaves to receive tips. If a slave saved his tips, he might one day be able to buy his freedom from his master. Julius Caesar was known for being a "big tipper," and it was not uncommon for him, if he had been served well at a dinner party by one of his friend's slave girls (or boys) to inquire at the end of the party as to how much that slave needed in order to buy his freedom, and then leave that amount as a gratuity!

Watch Out—Don't Forget to Pay your Tuition!

The term "tuition" is a very specific word, if you think about it. We all have "bills" to pay. There's the gas bill, the electric bill, etc. You've got your mortgage "payment," just as you probably have a car "payment." We get all sorts of credit card "statements," that ask us to "remit" what we owe. But the word "tuition" is reserved for one particular financial transaction, and that's the money you pay to go to school. The Latin root for this noun is the same one as for the word "tutor" that we mentioned above as a very, *very* expensive alternative to sending your kid off to a school in Athens (which was expensive enough!). We use the word "tutor" almost as synonymous with "teacher," because they both derive from the Latin verb *tueri*, which means, literally, "to look out for" or "watch over." It's just another instance of how the words associated with school all share a common theme, and that is "protection."

We perhaps see this meaning in the word "intuition," which has nothing to do with school, but everything to do with having the ability to "watch out for" what's coming around the next corner in life. It, too, is a very protective term, and that is why the root is so prevalent when it comes to words relating to school.

It's All "Academic"

There was a public park near Athens just outside the city walls—to the north-west of the Dipylon gate—called the "Academy" (Ακαδαμια). It was named after a man named Academus who had been a hero in the Trojan War. Well, it was in the Academy, in this grove in this park that a man named Plato opened a school. It cost nothing to attend and anyone who wanted to attend could. Those who did attend—and among them was a man named Socrates—would practice debating different subjects. They would take turns taking sides. One guy would argue the "pro" side of the argument, and then they'd switch and he'd have to argue the "con" side of the same argument. It had nothing to do with who was right or wrong—there *was* no right or wrong—it was just an exercise in learning how to formulate a logical argument no matter what the issue was or how you felt about it.

Our phrase, "It's all academic," derives from the way Plato ran his school. To say something is just "academic" means that it is purely hypothetical and ultimately has no impact on anything. In the real world, if you make a mistake, shit happens. Cross the centerline—a matter of inches—and people die. If you are in the Academy, fooling around with theories and you get it wrong, you lose an argument—*nothing* happens! Nobody dies. The word "academy" first appears in English with the sense of any kind of school or place of learning around the year 1500, which seems pretty late for this particular word.

Hey, What's your Major?

There comes a time in every college student's life when he has to make that big decision to declare a major! There are so many to choose from, some people can't make up their minds. Biology? Anthropology? Sociology? Zoology? Computer Technology? Biotechnology? Ecology? Ever wonder why so many majors in college end in the suffix "logy?"

Words, Words, Words…

The Greeks had three different concepts of what a "word" was, and so had three different words to express them. They had μυθος (say: "moo-thos"), which was the "spoken" word. There was επος (say: "eh-pos"), which was the "written" word, and there was λογος (say: "loh-gos"), which was the "thought" word.

Now, if we transliterate all three words from the Greek alphabet into the Roman alphabet (which is what we use) we'll see that it is from their word for the "spoken" word (μυθος) that we get our word "myth," because myths were stories that people told to one another. If we do the same with the "written" word (επος), we get our word "epic" because epics were written down. And if we do the same for the "thought" word (λογος), we see it is where we get the word "logic" for describing the mental process.

While we get "logic" from λογος, we also get the root *log*, which we most often encounter as the suffix "logy," which means "the study of" whatever root it is spliced onto. Because all our students are so eagerly studying something, the names of so many of our subject are built using it!

Finally...Graduation!

Like the word "education," the word "graduation" also has the idea of "moving up" built into it. The root of the word is *grad,* and it derives from the Latin noun *gradus,* which means "step." When you "graduate," you move up to the next step, whatever that may be. Hence, the expression: "making the grade." Same root. And remember: you'll only graduate if you make good "grades!"

Bachelor Party!

If you do actually make it all the way to graduation, you will probably leave college as a "Bachelor" of "Something." The most common degrees awarded to undergraduates are the "Bachelor of Arts," (often referred to as a "B.A."), and the "Bachelor of Science," (otherwise known by its initials as a "B.S.").

The "arts" and the "science" parts are easy enough to understand, but the term "bachelor" has a curious history behind it. It wasn't until relatively recently that "bachelor" came to be used specifically for men who were not yet married, with the implication that they were certainly of the age when they could—and perhaps even *should*—be hitched. In fact, it hasn't always been used exclusively of men. In his play *The Magnetic Lady* (1632), Ben Johnson used it when referring to an unmarried woman!

Our word "bachelor" dates back to at least the beginning of the fourteenth century. One theory is that it derives from the Latin words *baca* (which was their term for the fruit of the olive tree), and *laureates,* (an adjective meaning "wearing the laurel crown"). The term *bacalaureatus* would mean, then, "one crowned with olive branches." This is not so far off the mark. Victorious athletes in ancient Greece received such crowns as a symbol of their achievement.

But to this day, at least in the world of academics, we speak of a "baccalaureate degree" as often as we do a "bachelor's degree." The word "bachelor," though it started out as a purely academic term, came to be used specifically of men probably because, until relatively recently, it was only men who ever got a college education. Once they did, they started to climb the social ladder quite quickly, which made them targets for women who could support themselves only through menial servitude and therefore were desperately looking for husbands (read: "mealtickets") to support them.

Etymological Note: Often people who get the "B.S." make jokes about the initials of the degree being identical to "BS," those we use when referring to something as "bullshit." We say things like, "That's just BS, don't pay attention to it." People who "fling or sling the bull" are known as "BS artists." The word "bullshit" is first recorded in 1914 (a letter from James Joyce to Ezra Pound: "I enclose a prize sample of bullshit.") In truth, it is probably older than that, as our word "shit" may go all the way back to the Indo-European root *skei* which means "to divide." It makes its appearance in Old English as *scitan,* meaning "to defecate." Literally, it means "to divide and cut waste from our body, to separate it from us." So one really can't "take" a "shit," but one can certainly "leave" one. As American slang meaning "nonsense" or "lies," it is hard to tell which came first, "shit" or "bullshit" because the expression "bull" is first recorded around 1850, during the time of the Civil War—but who gives a shit anyway?

Saying Farewell

For high school graduates, the next step may be college. For college grads, it may be "graduate school." Regardless, at either celebration, you're going to have to sit through a "valediction" delivered by the class "valedictorian." The term comes from the Latin root *vale*, which is actually the imperative form of the verb *valere* and means "be well!" and the root *dict* which comes from the Latin verb *dicere*, which means "to say." So, a "valediction" is any form of a farewell address.

But if you listen to enough of them, you start to realize that if a valediction is well written, if it does what everyone expects it to do, then it not only says "good-bye" to the four (or five or six…) years you spent drinking beer and sleeping with each other, but it should also "say hello" to the future, to the next four, five or six years you're going to spend drinking beer and sleeping with other people!

The fact that so many "valedictions" end up saying both "goodbye" (to the past) as well as "hello" (to the future) may not be simply a coincidence. The Latin verb *vale*, meaning "to be well," need not have only been used in ancient Roman society to say farewell. It could have easily been used as a greeting as well, if we simply don't understand it as being used only in its imperative (i.e., as a command) form. Watch as two ancient Romans meet on the street:

| Marcus : "*Ecce Lucius*! *Vales*?" ("Yo, Lucius! How's it going?") |
| Lucius : "*Valeo, Marcus, et tu?*" ("Well, Marcus, and you?") |

It's really a no brainer. This would explain why all "valedictions" contain both messages—why they say both "goodbye" and "hello." Now, why they seem to go *on* and *on* and *on* is another question all together!

Getting your Walking Papers!

Finally, it arrives! It is The Big Day. You get to hear your name called out and you walk across that stage and get that piece of paper that says You Did It! You're going to get your "diploma!"

The word "diploma" comes from the Latin *diploma*, directly into English completely unchanged. The Romans stole it from the Greeks (διπλωμα). Literally, the word means something "folded twice." A "diploma" in the ancient world was a folded document or hinged writing tablet containing instructions given by a magistrate to assure free passage and assistance to the bearer on his journey.

The first use of the word in English in its modern sense of "academic diploma" was in 1682. Like "matriculation," it's also a nice metaphor for the document that you will receive before you start out on the great journey of your life.

The Body Eclectic I

Anatomy 101

For as far back as we can trace recorded history, man has been interested in exploring the anatomy of the human body. By as early as around 3000 B.C., the ancient Egyptians had already developed a highly sophisticated process called "mummification" for the preservation of the body for the afterlife. During mummification, most of the internal organs were expertly removed, but beyond stuffing them into canopic jars, the Egyptians didn't seem to have been all that keen on learning what made them tick.

Some 2000 years later, when barbarians from northern Europe and the southern steppes of Russia, began periodically invading Greece during the late Bronze Age, many an enemy warrior expressed great interested in "exploring" the internal organs of the Greeks—only they used their spears and swords to do it! But just like the Egyptians before them, once they got in there they kind of lost interest in any scientific application to their effort. In other words, they didn't take any notes! It wasn't until the fifth century B.C. during the Golden Age of ancient Greek culture, that the Greeks themselves finally began to take a serious interest in a scientific study of the human body.

The way the Greeks approached the study of human anatomy was to hang around the sidelines of a battlefield and wait for the fighting to stop. Once it did—and everyone who could, had ridden, run, walked, stalked, slinked, or as best they could, crawled away—they would go to work, stalking the corpses of the fallen warriors, looking for some luckless bastard who was not *quite* dead yet, but who had been overlooked and left behind by his retreating "brothers-in-arms." Often they'd find more than one, but hey—the more the merrier!

Digging in!

If we dissect the word "anatomy," we can see that it is made up of the Greek root *tom* (τομ) meaning "to cut," and the prefix "ana" (ανα). Now, as we have seen with Latin prefixes, Greek prefixes operate in much the same way—generally showing direction (up/down; over/under; before/after; etc.) or negation. Also, like Latin prefixes, they can mean different things depending on the root to which they are attached, and the general context of the word in the sentence. With the root *tom*, in this context, the prefix "ana" means "up." So "anatomy" means, literally, "cutting up."

> **Etymological Note:** While in the present context of the word "anatomy," the prefix "ana" means "up." In another context, it can mean "back" as well. These two meanings may seem to us today to have little in common with each other, but to an ancient Greek, the two were inseparable. If you have ever been to Greece, then you know it is a very rocky, mountainous place. Because of the nature of its terrain—aside from a few olive groves and vineyards—there was very little arable land available for farming. As a result, the primary source of subsistence for the Greeks came from the sea. For this reason, the ancient Greeks were very skilled fishermen (as they still are today). But because it was unsafe to live by the seashore due to the ever present threat of attack by marauding bands of pirates, most Greek villages were located several miles inland. Every day the fishermen would leave their homes and go "down" (κατα = *cata*) to the sea where their ships were moored. At the end of the day, with the fishing done, it was time to go "back." And because the walk inland was also a journey uphill from sea level, "ana" means both "up" as well as "back.."

Anything Moving in There?

Imagine fighting all day long in the hot sun, throwing spears and dodging swords, and then—SLAM!—you take one in the chest and—BOOM!—down you go like a sack of shit. So you're lying there, waiting for the next ferry to The Underworld to come along and carry you across the River Styx—when all of a sudden these *people* appear from out of nowhere, drag you off into the woods, cut you open with a dull knife, and start scooping out your lungs with a rusty spoon!

It wasn't that the ancient Greeks were sadistic monsters—they saw themselves as *scientists*. The object of the game, as it were, was to get their hands on someone who was still alive so that when they cut him open, the organs inside would still be *moving*. This way they could poke around and observe how the organs worked in order to determine their function. As soon as they realized that once the guy's *organs* stopped moving, so did *the guy*, it must have occurred to them that whatever was moving in there had to be *important!* This was why getting in there while the guy was still alive was of such consequence. And because all the stuff that was still moving—like the lungs and the heart—was clustered together in the body cavity, the Greeks quickly arrived at the conclusion that this central part of the body housed the most important parts of a man.

Central Housing

The Greeks called this part of the body—what they considered to be the center of a man, where all the important stuff was—the *phrēn* (φρην—say: "frane"), and it encompassed the whole area of the abdominal cavity. It was here that these early Greeks determined that the "essence" of a man resided—it was the home of his soul, the seat of his emotions, the origin of his thoughts, etc. All the important ingredients that made up a man were all right in there—in the *phrēn*—or so they thought because that was where all the stuff that was moving seemed to be.

The root *phrēn* applies to anything having to do with this part of the body. In our vernacular, because when transliterated into the Roman alphabet, *phrēn* becomes *frēn*, we get words like "frenzy" and "frenetic"—words that have come to describe someone who is acting emotionally, under the influence of his *phrēn* (through "vowel shortening" we also get "frantic"). These words carry with them the implication that someone who is in a "frenzy," who is acting "frenetic," is not in control of his *emotions*—his *emotions* are in control of *him*. And that was a big time no-no because the ancient Greeks believed that being controlled by your emotions, as opposed to using your rational thoughts to control *them*, was dangerous, and seldom, if ever, led to anything good. This uniquely Greek view of the human condition is key to understanding how the ancient Greeks viewed both themselves and the world in which they lived.

Going "Schizo"

The Greek verb *schizo* (σχιζω—say: "skidso") means "to split" or "cut." So, if we add "*schizo*" as a prefix to the root *phrēn,* we have built the word "schizophrenic," which literally means having a "split *phrēn*." But because the *phrēn* was the foundation of a man's identity, having a split *phrēn* was *not* a good thing and was generally used to describe someone with a "split personality"—someone who may have acted one way yesterday, may act another way today, and god only knows what the hell he's going to do tomorrow. In severe cases of schizophrenia, the emotional mood swings can change from hour to hour, or even minute to minute. Medical terminology—like all words—changes over time. Today, the fashionable term for "split personality" is "Multiple Personality Disorder" or, simply, MPD.

Psych 101

Packed up in your *phrēn*, along with everything else, was something the Greeks called the ψυχη (psyche—say: "psoo-kay"). The ψυχη was not an "organ" you could see or touch—like the gall bladder or the pancreas—rather, it was a "force," something the Greeks considered to be what we might call the "soul" of the man. We might find it easier to grasp this concept when we see the word in its transliterated form of *psyche*. The fact that in today's academic vernacular the term "psychology" means the "study of the mind" reinforces the idea that the Greeks believed that everything of importance in a man resided in his *phrēn*. The most important were his mental processes, but this applied to his emotions as well, leading to a constant tension between one's "emotional self" and one's "rational self."

Gray Matter

Today, we couldn't ever imagine the notion that we think with our stomachs (although, judging by some people's eating habits you might assume that some of us do!). But if no one had ever told you that you thought with your brain, how would you know that you did?

Today, however, thanks to centuries of medical study and research, we know that the mental process takes place in the brain and that the brain is the dominant organ of the central nervous system. The central nervous system is a vast network of neurons and transmitters that controls just about every move we make. So in order to run this system, the brain has had to develop over ten thousand million nerve cells! And yet the brain itself has no capacity for sensation—it feels no pain whatsoever—even if jabbed through an incision in the skull! So when they got around to cutting open the skulls of the *I'm Not Dead Yet!* club, and started poking and probing the big, round, mass of grey matter they found inside, they would have gotten little if any reaction from their "subject" whatsoever.

So what other conclusion could those early Greek "physicians" have arrived at other than that the brain was not a very important organ at all? It certainly could not be as important as anything they found squirming around inside the *phrēn*. Because when all that stuff *stopped* moving, their "subject" *stopped* moving, too! All of a sudden, he was *dead*. But that stuff inside the skull, it was never even moving to *begin* with. And when they jabbed it with a stick or something, they got no reaction from the guy when he was still living. So how important could it be?

The Radiator Theory

But they knew that the brain *had* to do *something*, right? What they came up with might surprise you, but understanding that the blood circulated though it, and seeing that the brain was up there at the top of the body, with little else but the skull and some hair to shield it from the heat of the summer sun and the chill of a winter night's wind, it followed to reason that the temperature of the blood was directly affected by the temperature of the brain. So, a hot brain would result in warm blood, and a cold brain, cold blood.

Because we humans are classified as a "warm blooded" species, our bodies have to have some mechanism for maintaining a constant body temperature. So it occurred to them that the brain—by virtue of its placement at the top of the head, and perhaps, because it didn't move like the other organs did, and on top of all that, seemed to have no feeling—was uniquely designed to do just this: maintain the temperature of the body by maintaining the temperature of the blood. If a Greek failed to cover his head while toiling under the hot Mediterranean sun and died of heatstroke, it was because his blood "overheated."

Likewise, say, if while hunting stags along the wintry slopes of the Thracian mountains a Greek suffered frostbite, or even froze to death, it was due to the fact that his headgear—if he was even *wearing* any to begin with—had been insufficient to keep the brain warm enough to keep his blood warm. From what we know today, this sounds entirely preposterous, but didn't your mother ever remind you to wear your knit cap when you went out to play in the snow because you lost about sixty-percent of your body heat through your head? *Mine* certainly did!

Let's Get Physical

In the previous chapter, we saw how the word "doctor" by itself has nothing to do with the medical profession. The original term was "medical doctor," and the "medical" part just dropped off. "Doctor" is a word based on the Latin root meaning "to teach." But the word "physician" is a Greek word and its root, *physic* (φυσικ), means "nature" and connotes anything in its "natural state." So these guys—out there in the aftermath of the battle, looking for the wounded to dissect so they could observe the organs in their "natural state"—these would become the first true "physicians." Which *is* a "medical" word, for human beings, like dogs and cats and every other thing in the universe—from a gall bladder to a black hole—is part of what we call "nature."

> **Etymological Note:** There really is no difference, by the way, between the words "physician" and "physicist." They're both built on the same root, they just have different endings, both of which make the words nouns and both of which carry the meaning of "one who." The technical term is "occupational suffix." A "physician" deals with the human body in its natural state, and a "physicist" deals with, well, everything else in *its* natural state.

The Body Eclectic

When these early "physicians" began cutting open bodies and observing all that stuff in there squirming around, the first thing they had to do was give names to everything. This gave them a way they could talk to each other about what they were seeing—so they could take notes. They were essentially creating a whole new vocabulary, and as we'll see, many of the names they came up with were often taken from things they saw in the world that resembled things they saw in the human body. For example, the word for our windpipe, "trachea," is a direct transliteration of *tracheia* (τραχεια), a Greek adjective that means "rough." When the Greeks got round to naming it, because it felt "rough," that's what they named it. Reach up and feel your own trachea and you'll see they got the vocabulary right!

Our word "vocabulary" comes from the Latin *vocabularius*, and both words derive from the root *voca*, which means "to call." We encountered it in Chapter Four with the word "vocation." In this chapter and the next two, we'll take a look at what those Greeks, and also the Romans (who got into the "name game" as well) came up with when they started naming the different parts of the body. What we'll find is that because the Greeks and the Romans spoke different languages, yet each shared an intense interest in exploring and naming the various parts of the human body and figuring out how they functioned, what we end up with is one eclectic jumble of anatomical vocabulary!

> **Historical Note:** The word "eclectic" comes from the Greek *eklekticos* (εκλεκτικος), an adjective that means "having the quality or characteristic of being selective, of picking and choosing." The notion was taken up by Greek philosophers in the second century B.C., and it soon became its own branch of philosophy. The "Eclectics" flourished for a time in ancient Athens. They called their movement "Eclecticism" because they believed in picking and choosing from other schools of philosophy what they would and would not believe.

The "Name Game"

In the book of "Genesis," one of the first jobs that God gives to Adam is to name all the creatures of the earth—and what a job it must have been! At that point, *nothing* had a name. Adam must have been a busy guy! Today, we've got well over a million scientific names just for animals, about the same number for insects, and well over seven million for natural elements and man-made chemical compounds! That's a lot of vocabulary!

> **Statistical Note**: The United States Patent Office has over 350,000 names as registered trademarks. *The Oxford English Dictionary* contains over 450,000 words, while *Webster's Second International Dictionary* records some 650,000! Shakespeare's complete works contain somewhere around 25,000—the same number of words as you'll find in your average Sunday edition of the *New York Times*! It took about 6,000 words for King James to set down his version of *The Bible*. Combine all that with slang, jargon, borrowings from other languages and—let's not forget!— what's happening on the "hip-hop" scene—and linguists estimate that the English language now has between 15 and 20 million words in circulation! And yet, the average person has a working vocabulary of only about 2,800 words, while an above average individual's vocabulary can get as high as 60,000. How many words do *you* know?

Of course, we won't be able to cover the names of all the bones, organs, muscles, tendons, ligaments, glands, nerves, teeth, roots, veins, arteries, cells—and god knows what else we've got in these bodies of ours! For example, the human skeleton alone is made up of two-hundred and six bones. But what's interesting is that of all the bones in the human body, over half of them are located in the hands and the feet alone. Why do you suppose that is? Think about it next time you get on the treadmill at your local gym.

Etymological Note: The word "gym," as most people are aware, is short for "gymnasium," which is an exact transliteration of the Greek work *gymnasium* (γυμνασιον). The Greek verb to "work out" is γυμναζω (say: "goom-nah-dsow") and is built on the Greek stem *gymn* (γυμν), which means, literally, "to be naked." So a "gymnasium" is, literally, "a place where you go to be naked." That's because Greek athletes worked out in the nude. In fact, for many years, the athletes who competed in the Olympic Games did the same. Because of this, if a married woman was caught watching the Olympic Games, the punishment was death! On the other hand,, unmarried virgins between the ages of twelve and fourteen were bused in by the wagonloads to watch. The idea was that this was their opportunity to see the male form in its most perfect state—a chance to see what they had to look forward to. Then, six months later their fathers married them off to some fat old farmer, and it was game over. For many years, the Olympics were conducted in this way—in the nude, that is—until one year, a sprinter from Thrace was competing and he had—how shall we put it?—a somewhat larger endowment than his fellow competitors. So in order to keep his "endowment" from banging around his knees while he ran, he tied it up in a leather thong. The other Greeks thought this was hilarious—until he *won*! Suddenly, at the next Olympics, *all* the runners showed up wearing similar thongs and next thing you know?—the jock strap was born!

The Body Eclectic II

CHAPTER 8

The Human Hand

It is said that of all the shapes in the universe, the most challenging for an artist to depict is the human hand. Michelangelo was fascinated by this extraordinary appendage. Nor was he was alone in his fascination, as both he and his close contemporary and fellow Florentine, Leonardo DaVinci, did countless studies, sketches, casts, and sculptures of this remarkable instrument—let's not forget, after all, that it was the versatility of the hand that set old *Homo Habilis* apart from the rest of the monsters in the jungle, and was probably responsible for the survival of our species. It has been said that nearly everything man has invented—from the first spear to the "Saturday Night Special," to long range cruise missile—is nothing more than an extension of his hand.

Let's take a good look at Michelangelo's *David*, on view at the *Galleria dell'Accademia* in Florence, Italy. One of the most striking features of the sculpture is how Michelangelo portrayed David's *hands*. Examine them and you'll notice that they're deliberately out of proportion to the rest of his body. They are slightly too large. This was a conscious choice on Michelangelo's part—intended to show through the size of his hands that David was still but a youth, that he had yet to grow into them. Just as the paws of a puppy appear too big for his body, so Michelangelo gave David "puppy paws." Those oversize hands of his are a symbol not only of David's youth, but they also hold—in addition to the rock and slingshot with which he is about to fell the giant Goliath—the promise of his emerging manhood and subsequent leadership of his people.

Both the hands and the feet, as we mentioned in the previous chapter, contain over half the bones in the human body. Both share remarkable similarities, not only in their appearance and relative size, but also in the vocabulary that the ancient Greeks chose to describe their components. So for the sake of "expediency" (pun *intended*), we'll take a cursory look at some of the names of the bones of the human hands and feet, keeping in mind—because at one point we walked about on all four of them—that many of their bones share the same names.

A "Hands-On" Approach

The twenty-seven bones of the hand are connected by thirty- seven muscles, most of which control the movement of the fingers. The hand consists of five fingers—unless you consider the thumb to be something other than a "finger," which some anthropologists do because not all creatures with "fingers" have "thumbs," and we supposedly didn't get them until old *Homo Hablis* came along.

> **Etymological Note:** The word "muscle" has an interesting etymology of its own. If we break it down into its original elements, we get the Latin noun *mus* + the suffix "cle." The suffix "cle" is a contraction of the diminutive suffix "cule." A "diminutive suffix" makes whatever root it's attached onto "small." For example, the word "molecule" comes from the Latin word *moles* meaning "mass" or "pile," and "cule" meaning "small." So a "molecule" is literally a "small mass" or "pile" of matter. The word "muscle" comes from the Latin noun *mus*, which means "mouse," and the diminutive suffix "cle." The word "muscle" literally means "little mouse!" So if you want "bigger mice," so to speak, then you'd better get your lazy ass over to the γυμνασιον (just remember that nowadays, we keep our clothes *on*).

Each finger is made up of four bones. Starting from the base of the wrist and moving outward, the first bone, the longest and straightest, is called, simply, the "shaft"—an allusion no doubt to the technical term for the long straight section of a Greek column. Attached to the shaft of each finger are three smaller bones—each slightly shorter than the one preceding it—called, respectively, the "proximal," "middle," and "distal" *phalanx*. "Proximal," "middle," and "distal," are pretty self-explanatory: "nearest," "middle," and "farthest" (for "distal" just think of its cognate "distance" and you get the idea why they chose this term for the "farthest" bone of the finger). But "phalanx" is where things get interesting.

The Greek "phalanx" (φαλαγξ—say: "fay-lanks") is actually a military term for one of the most effective fighting machines on the planet from the seventh to the fourth century B.C. The *phalanx* was a series of columns of soldiers—at full strength ten men wide by ten deep—armed with long pikes, or *sarissae*. Similar to spears, they ranged in length from ten to fourteen feet. The men who filled the ranks of the *phalanx* were called *hoplites*, named after their *hoplon*, the large round shield they carried in addition to their spears.

The *phalanx* marched in a tight formation of parallel ranks. The men in the front ranks marched with their *sarissae* lowered and as a body the *phalanx* advanced deliberately and methodically toward the enemy. Those in the rear followed in step at their heels with their *sarissae* held aloft to deflect missiles and arrows. When one of the men in the front ranks went down in the fighting, the man behind him would lower his *sarissa* and step up to take his place.

So, it is easy to see how the Greeks saw the familiar "footprint" (get it?) of the Greek *phalanx* when they observed the bones of the feet and hands with their long parallel rows of bones arranged side by side in close proximity. Is it a coincidence that the Greek *phalanx* had the same number of ranks—ten—as we have fingers and toes? Maybe yes, maybe no…

Remember the Spartans!

Sparta, the most war-like of the Greek city-states, perfected the art of *phalanx* warfare. They were the hardest-core society in a world full of hard core societies. In Spartan culture, all male children were taken from their mothers at birth and raised by the state. The first thing the state did was expose every newborn male child on the side of a mountain for several days. Those few who survived were deemed to be the strongest and were trained to become the next generation of legendary Spartan warriors.

All Spartan boys were raised together, but apart from the rest of society—they lived, ate, and slept together in barracks—and underwent rigorous, daily military training. They were instructed in the use of the various weapons and tactics of Spartan warfare practically from the time they were old enough to walk. Because their entire youth was spent segregated not only from most other Spartan citizens, but particularly from the company of the opposite sex—and taught absolutely nothing about them—the companionship of other boys was the only form of intimacy they knew growing up. In fact, homosexual relationships between the youths was encouraged.

This type of "schooling," however, presented a serious problem when Spartan boys came of age to marry. Because for the previous eighteen years, their only experiences had been handling military equipment during the day, and "packing fudge" (while providing "reach-arounds") with their "bunkies," they had no idea what to do once they got between the sheets with someone who didn't have a dick, and were clueless about how to handle female equipment!

Cross Dressing Spartan Style

Suffice it to say that it was probably not uncommon, given his upbringing, for a young Spartan man to have trouble performing his marital duties on that first terrifying night. This was a big problem. Due to their culture's unique way of raising children by first exposing them, the mortality rate must have been huge. As a result, they needed young men to be able to impregnate their wives in order to produce more Spartans—and there was only *one* way to do that.

In order to resolve this problem, the state devised the following solution: on her wedding night, the bride would have her hair cut very short and styled after the fashion of all the other Spartan boys. Then they would substitute the traditional military tunic all boys grew up wearing for what would normally be the bride's wedding dress, so she would end up looking, more or less, like "one of the boys."

The idea was that once the lights went out, the groom would mount his new bride, but feeling the familiar attire of his former bunkmate, his instincts, honed over the past eighteen years, would take over and Mr. Mojo would manage to "put in" an appearance. This was a good start even if the new groom still "rode the caboose" until he began to figure out what that "other hole" was for—which for some men— Spartan or not—takes *years*, if not an entire *lifetime*—to figure out. Heck, some of us—even still today—have yet to figure out exactly what we're supposed to be doing down there!

Eventually, the Spartans must have come to terms with the "ins" and "outs" of the "heterosexual ritual," but they were never all that "into" it. Screwing your wife usually ran a distant second to an afternoon of playing "hide the pike" with the boys.

The Face that Launched a Thousand Ships

Helen, Queen of Sparta, who was said to have been the most beautiful woman on Earth, had the unlikely misfortune to be married to the King of Sparta, a short-tempered, wide little man named Menelaus. Now Menelaus might have been king of the most fearsome city-state in all of Greece, and when it came to spear chucking or sword waggling, he was without equal. But in the sack, he was putting Helen's feet to sleep.

So, one day this young stud named Paris shows up, and Helen runs off with him. Paris had a real reputation for being a ladies' man. He also just happened to be one of the sons of Priam, who was King of Troy. But none of that mattered. What mattered was that Paris, as a guest in Menelaus' house, stole Menelaus' wife virtually right out of their bedroom!

We're using the word "stole" here loosely. But whether or not she went willingly, her abduction amounted to an insult that no Greek could let go unredressed. So Menelaus, with the help of his brother

Agamemnon, persuaded all of the kings of Greece to muster their forces and launch a fleet across the Aegean Sea to sack Troy and bring Helen back. It was one of the single largest military operations ever mounted, and because of that, Helen came to be known as "the face that launched a thousand ships!"

The "Bird" is the Word!

Hands and their fingers are truly remarkable things. We've even developed a language that uses them to enable us to communicate with the deaf. "Sign language"—as it's called—can be an amazingly nuanced means of communication, considering what you've got to work with. So nuanced is this language, in fact, that you can even say "fuck you" with it. And so universal became the sign for "fuck you" that anyone—whether he had studied sign language or not—could both use it and understand it when he saw it directed at him.

To make the sign you simply need raise your middle finger (either hand will do), while keeping the other four tightly wrapped in a sort of fist. With your palm facing you, extend your arm upward and outward toward whomever you wish to be the recipient of the message. The common euphemism for this particular sign is "the finger" or "the bird." When you do it to someone, you are said to be "giving them the finger," or "flipping them the bird," or simply "flipping them off."

> **Etymological Note:** Once again, we can spot our old friend "pha" even when it is in disguise, as it so often is when we place a prefix on the front of it. In this case, the prefix is the Greek prefix "eu" (εʊ) which means "good." Now the "a" of the "pha" has changed to an "e" through "vowel shortening," thanks to the addition of the prefix "eu." So a "euphemism" is a polite way to put a good label on something that might not otherwise deserve it. For example, "Custodial Technician" would be a euphemism for a "janitor," and a "Personal Relaxation Therapist" would do nicely for "hooker".

Funny, but you don't get "flipped off" as much these days as you might have had you lived, say, back in the 1960's—during the Vietnam War, when protest marches and anti-war rallies were much more in fashion than they are today—when saying "fuck you" by flipping someone off was a very popular form of expression. The gesture itself has its own history that we can trace back to a time well before the 1960's. In fact, it goes all the way back to the first century after Christ, and maybe even before that.

Like Kissing your Sister

The emperor Caligula was a complete freak, a classic sociopathic, psychotic basket case who became emperor of Rome at the tender age of twenty-three or twenty-four—after having the Praetorian Guard suffocate his uncle Tiberius while he lay on his deathbed. Things went okay with Caligula for about the first six months of his reign, and then something went terribly awry, and he went completely haywire. Aside from having an affair with Drusilla, on of his sisters, he prostituted his other two and—according to some of our historical sources—his mother as well. He was also known for being very good at torturing his enemies, murdering his friends, and raping the wives of his senators. According to one source, Caligula once graciously threw a party for a young senator and his virgin bride to celebrate their marriage on their wedding night. At one point in the evening, the emperor, taking the young woman by the hand, excused himself and escorted her off to a private bedroom where he "broke her in," so to speak. He then returned to the dinner table and proceeded to critique her performance in front of her new groom and the rest of the dinner guests!

Kiss the "Birdie"

It was no secret that Caligula detested the senate, largely because it was the senate that tried to keep him from going completely apeshit. So just to *fuck* with their heads, as we discussed above, he had his horse, Incitatus, declared a senator! And to show even more contempt for them, whenever a senator would request an audience with the emperor, Caligula would make the senator kneel before him, and, extending his middle finger, command the senator to "kiss the birdie!" Caligula got a big kick out of this particular form of humiliation, but few senators shared the emperor's sense of humor, so it wasn't long before they hatched a plot to rid the empire of this lunatic.

Pissed Off

You could say Caligula really pissed off a lot of people—*literally*. One of his favorite things to do was to piss into the aqueducts leading into the various neighborhoods of Rome! Well, one day, while watching the chariot races in the Circus Maximus, nature called. So Caligula rose from his throne in the imperial box to take a leak. Accompanied by his trusted Praetorian Guard, whose job it was to protect the life of the emperor wherever he went, Caligula was jumped by a group of senators as he lifted his toga to drain his bladder. He was brutally stabbed to death while his trusted Praetorian Guards just looked the other way (or maybe even joined in). All in all, his time on the throne didn't last very long. He ruled Rome for only four chaotic years: from 37 to 41 A.D.

Watching your Peds & Pods

The Latin root for foot is *ped*; the Greek root is *pod* (ποδ). Now *ped* and *pod* would seem pretty easy to keep straight, and they usually are, until you learn that there is another Greek root that looks just like the Latin root *ped*. This one, though, comes from the Greek word παιδος (say: "pie-dos,"), and means "child." Only, through "vowel shortening," the Greek diphthong "αι" transliterates into English either as "ae" or "e," as we saw with the words "archaeology" and "archeology" in a previous chapter.

Take a Walk

The word "pedestrian," as a noun, means one who travels by foot. Simple enough. But it can also be used as an adjective with the pejorative meanings of "common" or "low-life." These meanings derive, I think, from perhaps the idea that only the poorest of the poor, the Great Unwashed, as they're sometimes called, had to travel "by foot." It was only those with a certain amount of sophistication, education, and therefore money, who could afford a horse, a chariot, a wagon, etc.

With all these "peds" and "pods" wandering around, we can get really tangled up when we start talking about words like "pediatrician." The Greek noun for "medical doctor" is *iatros* (ιατρος—say: "ee-ah-tros"), though we usually encounter it as the suffix "–iatrician." So, because the word "pediatrician" is *not* built on the Latin root for "foot" (*ped*) but on the Greek root for "child" (*ped*), it therefore does not mean "foot doctor," but "children's doctor." If we wanted to make the word for "foot doctor," we would use the Greek root for foot (*pod*) and come up with the term "podiatrist."

What's the Story?

Greek and Roman mythology had basically one story for the creation of *Everything*; But the problem with *all* mythologies is that because they're passed orally from generation to generation, we end up with many different versions of the same story. We'll try to unpack the various accounts of *The Story* of the creation of Greece and Rome in later chapters, but for now we can start off with a little background on Zeus.

Zeus, who would go on to become the King of the Greek Olympian gods, was born into a very dysfunctional family. His father, Cronos, was part of the generation of gods known as the Titans. These were a race of giants who preceded the Olympian gods, of which Zeus was a member.

Pedophagy, Anyone?

Now, Cronos' father, Uranus, had a bad case of "pedophagy" and had a hard time keeping it under control. What was Uranus' problem? If we break down the word, we get: *ped • o • phagy*. The root *ped* comes from the Greek word for "child," and the suffix "phagy" comes from the Greek verb *phagein* (φαγειν—say: "fah-gain"), meaning "to eat." Notice how the verb *phagein* has "swallowed" our old friend, the root *pha*! Just a coincidence? I doubt it.

So what's old Uranus up to? He's *eating* his *children*! His wife, Gaia, tried everything to get him to kick the habit. She thought maybe it was her cooking, so she took a course in gourmet Greek cuisine. But even her best *spanakopita* couldn't keep Uranus off the hard stuff. She even got him to attend some meetings of "Pedophagists Anonymous," but the cure never took.

> **Zoological Note:** As we see, pedophagy isn't a fancy name for a "foot fetish." (that would be "podophagy"). And it usually doesn't mean eating just any old children but eating one's *own* children! As bizarre as this sounds, however "pedophagy" is something that *still* goes on in the world today, only usually not among humans. When *that* happens, it's called something else—a *felony*! But it does exist in nature—in the animal world, among certain reptiles, birds, insects, and even some mammals it can be quite common.

So, Uranus is munching his way through the family tree when word comes down that Cronos is next. Cronos does what any kid would do in his situation: he goes running to his mother—who is altogether aware of the problem and not at all pleased with her husband's behavior. The two of them put their heads together and come up with a plan.

The Plan

The plan was to have Cronos hide in their bedroom, near the bed, behind the drapes. Then, later that night when Uranus comes in to mount Gaia for a little "boom-boom" time, Cronos jumps out from behind the curtains, whips out his dagger, and strikes. Well, that was the plan, anyway. But it was dark in there and Cronos was no doubt nervous and so instead of driving the blade through his evil father's back, he somehow manages to slice off his dad's genitals—the full package—the whole nine yards, so to speak (and being a god of the race of the giants, nine yards was probably a pretty accurate description.)

Uranus eventually died from his wounds, and Cronos succeeded to the throne. As for his severed cock and balls, Cronos threw these out the window. They landed in the Mediterranean sea and swirled around in the churning surf until, as legend has it, out of all that sea foam mess sprang the goddess Aphrodite, surfing on a half-shell. Given the circumstances surrounding her creation, it should come as no surprise that she became the Goddess of Sex!

Masters of the Universe

When Zeus finally came to inherit the throne, he and his brothers—Poseidon and Pluto—drew lots to see who would rule the different parts of the universe. Zeus won the draw and became the ruler of the sky, Poseidon got the sea, and Pluto became ruler of The Underworld. Since they made their homes on Mt. Olympus, they became known as the Olympian gods.

Zeus may have had the most power of the three, but Pluto became the wealthiest because it was customary in ancient Greece to place coins over the eyes of the dead before they went on their journey to The

Underworld. And even though he had to share a cut of the take with Charon, the ferryman who carried the dead across the River Styx, over the years that still added up to a chunk of change! Pluto's name became associated with wealth; hence our term "plutocrat," which is used to describe a person who is powerful because of his money.

A Feast Fit for the Gods

Perhaps the most famous story involving pedophagy is that of the House of Atreus. According to legend, Tantalus one day decided to invite the Olympian gods to a dinner party to try out a little experiment. He wanted to see if they were as smart as they were cracked up to be. In order to test their omniscience, he had his son, Pelops, cut up into little pieces and cooked into a stew which he then fed to the gods thinking that he could fool them into eating the human flesh. Having ordered his cooks to use the Extra Spicy Hot Sauce, he was certain that there was *no way* they would know.

They Knew

Why he chose his own son to conduct his little experiment is one of those family secrets that we'll just never know. But for his crime, Tantalus was banished to The Underworld and because of the nature of his offense was kept in a state of perpetual hunger and thirst. They made him stand in a stream of cool, mineral enriched spring water that rose all the way up to his chin, while hanging down right above his head were the boughs of rich, ripe, fruit trees. But every time he tilted his head down to get a drink, the stream dried up; and whenever he attempted to reach up and grab an apple or a pear or something— *anything*—a sudden strong breeze would blow the branches up out of his reach. Hence our word "tantalizing," which we use to describe something (or someone) that we desperately desire but can never have! As for his son, Pelops, the gods took pity on him and had him put back together again.

The Fall of the House of Atreus

Pelops went on to have two sons, Atreus and Thyestes. But because of what Tantalus had done, there was a curse over the entire family line. They say some afflictions skip a generation? Well, not in *this* case!

Both Atreus and Thyestes naturally wanted to inherit the throne. But since Atreus was the first-born son, the old rule of "primogeniture" kicked in and so it was he who got to wear the crown. This pissed Thyestes off, so in order to get back at Atreus, Thyestes seduced Atreus' wife, Aerope. When Atreus found out about the affair, he was so enraged that he "cooked up" a scheme to have his revenge!

Atreus doesn't let Thyestes know that *he* knows about the affair. Instead, he invites Thysestes and his children over to the palace one night for dinner under the pretext of wanting to make peace between them. What was the big beef, anyway? So he got to be king because he was first-born? What could *he* do about it? Why could they not simply bury the hatchet? They were, after all, brothers! Couldn't they just get along?

This was the line Atreus sold his brother, and Thyestes bought it all the way. The next night, Thyestes shows up with two of his three sons (Aegisthus, his eldest, was away at school and couldn't make it). So while Atreus is entertaining Thyestes, getting him all liquored up with goblets of the old vino, the two young boys get led away into the kitchen. This would not have aroused any suspicion, as it was customary for children and adults to dine separately. But when the children arrive in the kitchen, Atreus' servants slaughter them, slice their flesh up into little pieces and cook them into the meal.

Seconds, Anyone?

Later, as a somewhat drunk and jolly Thyestes is gobbling down his second helping of the ghastly, grizzly gruel, and waxing sentimental about how good it was to be tight with his brother again—with a forkful of little Thyestes Jr. still in his mouth!—Atreus reveals what he has done! Thyestes has just eaten his own children! Thyestes leaves the palace in ruin and shame, but as he does he places a curse on the house of Atreus, and vows that his surviving son, Aegisthus, will have his revenge!

The ultimate crime, in the eyes of the gods, was to eat *your own* children—whether you were aware of it or not. Unfortunately, the penultimate crime was to kill someone *else's* children and feed them to *their* parents. Either way, it set in motion cycles of retribution and retaliation that would keep the Greek Tragedians Aeschylus, Sophocles, and Euripides in business for a long time!

 Etymological Note: The word "penultimate" comes from the Latin adverb *paene*, which means "nearly" or "almost" and the adjective *ultimus*, meaning "last" or "final." The diphthong "ae" in *paene* becomes the "e" in "pen" through "vowel shortening." So the word "penultimate" means, literally, "almost" or "next to the last." We encounter it on a more regular basis with the word "peninsula," which comes from *paene* + *insula*, the Latin word for "island." A "peninsula" is a land formation that is "nearly an island." Just think Florida.

Even Julius Caesar Had a Vagina!

Probably several! One of the strangest stories to come out of the etymology of the human body is that of the word "vagina." "Vagina" is actually a Latin term for a piece of Roman military equipment issued to every solder in the Roman army. In Latin, *vagina* means "sheath" or "scabbard," and a Roman solder wore it on a belt around his waist and used it to carry his sword. But you can see the metaphor at work here: a *vagina*, by virtue of its shape and the fact that it was designed to accommodate a long, straight object of some girth, was the perfect word for that part of the female anatomy that was designed to do pretty much the same thing.

But what is strange about all this is that, if they chose the word *vagina* as the name for that specific part of the female anatomy that could accommodate something long and "sword-like," you would think—if only to preserve the metaphor—that they would have chosen the corresponding Latin word for that particular piece of equipment that went *inside* the *vagina*—namely the *gladius!* The Roman *gladius* was a long, heavy sword—a thick piece of steel that often took two hands to wield. But is that the name *we* get for what *we* put inside the *vagina*? Not even *close*. We don't get the word for "sword."—we don't even get the word for *dagger*! The word those bastards stuck us with was *penis*. We got stuck with a *penis!*—which is the Latin word for "little tail." Little tail, such as you would find on a little doggie! Sorry, fellas, but you just can't make this shit up.!

> **Literary Note:** If you ever get a chance to read Julius Caesar's account of the Gallic Wars in Latin, the celebrated *Bellum Gallicum*, you will find the word "vagina" on almost every other page. Soldiers are always losing their "vaginas," or dropping their "vaginas" in the mud, or if they've lost their sword, hitting the enemy on the head with their "vaginas."

The "Moveable Womb"

Either those ancient physicians encountered some female warriors out there on the battle field or else they came up with this theory born of years upon years of pure frustration from dealing with the opposite sex! They called it the "moveable womb" theory. They actually believed that the womb moved around inside the *phrēn* of a woman's body, and that this accounted for the mood swings of their wives!

It worked like this: when the womb was down in place, between a woman's thighs, *then* the woman was fertile and she could conceive. More importantly, you could *reason* with the *bitch*! But it resided there for only a short time during the month. The rest of the time, they theorized that the womb actually moved around inside the *phrēn*, and that this accounted for all the different temperaments that they had to deal with, month in and month out!

 Etymological Note: The Latin root for "month" is *menstra*. From it, we get words in Latin like *menstruum*, which is the term for a "monthly payment," and the adjective *menstrualis*, meaning "occurring on a monthly basis." It is also the root of "menstruation," which means, literally, "monthing."

The Body Eclectic III

Eye, Ears, Nose & Throat

Aside from housing the brain—which by now we know is not a "radiator" that controls the temperature of the blood, but rather the control center for the entire Central Fucking Nervous System—the head also feeds the brain with sensory input from the outside world. To do this, contained in the cavity of the skull are all the body's main sensory organs: the eyes, the ears, the olfactory nerves in the nose, and the taste buds along the surface membrane of the tongue.

The only other sense we have is not connected to a particular organ, such as the eye or the nose, rather it is a systemic "sense" that sends impulses to the brain through the central nervous system. We usually associate this sense with the hand, which we discussed in some detail in the preceding chapter. Hence, this sense is referred to as our "tactile" sense—if we can touch something, we often use the word "tangible" from the Latin verb *tangere*, meaning "to touch." It is therefore safe to say that the hand is the primary organ for any "tangible" purposes we have—not to mention its "recreational purposes!"

The head has seven openings that allow these organs to feed the brain: the two orbital socket of the eyes, which allow us to see; the ears, which allow sound waves into the brain; the two nostrils, which allow us to smell as well as draw breath (the object of the game!); and the mouth, which also helps us to take in oxygen, as well as nourishment but—and perhaps most important of all—it also allows us to form words.

Etymological Note: The word "face" comes from the Latin word *facies*, where *fa* is once again the root. The mouth, the largest opening in the face, is perhaps also the most important, because not only is it through the mouth that food enters the body through the eso*pha*gus—but it is also with the mouth that we form words!

If we were to slice the head right down the middle of the nose into two equal sections—as no doubt those early Greek "physicians" did out there on the battlefield—we would see that all of these "sensory" organs in the head are connected by a vast series of cavities located right behind the nose called the "sinuses."

Sartorial Note: The word "sinus" comes directly from the Latin word *sinus*, and it is the term for the deep fold in the Roman toga that Roman statesmen would cradle in their left arm. It was a status symbol. With fine, hand-spun wool being an expensive commodity in Rome, the larger the toga, the deeper the *sinus*—and the deeper the *sinus*, the deeper the pockets of its wearer.

It is through the "sinuses" that the sensory organs in our head are connected. Our noses drain through our sinuses, our sinuses connect to the eyes so that we can produce tears. Our tears flow out of our "lacrimal ducts"—*lacrima* being the Latin word for tear—which are extensions of the "nasolacrimal duct" that also hooks up to the sinuses. Even the ears are connected to the sinuses through the "Eustachian tube," which serves to equalize air pressure on either side of the eardrums. If you've ever held your nose shut and tried to blow real hard, more than likely your ears would stop up. That's also why, if you've ever had a sinus infection, the early symptoms can range from an earache or a toothache to pressure around or behind the nose and eyes.

Your ears are the organs that not only allow you to hear, but also keep your balance as you move around in the world. The ear has three basic parts: the outer ear, which is the part that sticks out of the side of the head and by its shape is designed to "catch" as much sound as it can and funnel it into the head; the middle ear contains three "ossicles"(from *ossa*, the Latin word for "bone," plus the diminutive suffix "cle") that are responsible for conveying sound to the inner ear; and the inner ear is where we find the "Eustachian tube" which provides the ear's link to the sinuses. The inner ear receives its signals from the middle ear and then sends them as electrical impulses to the brain. It is also the inner ear that houses the "labyrinth," a tiny bone and membrane mechanism that controls the body's sense of balance. This particular part of the ear is called the "labyrinth" because it is a tiny, protected chamber in the center of the innermost part of the ear.

The First Labyrinth

The first labyrinth was built at Knossos, on the island of Crete, to house the Minotaur, a monster with the body of a man, the head of a bull, and a voracious appetite that was only satisfied by the sacrifice of seven virgin boys and seven virgin girls imported annually from Athens. It can't get much weirder than that, can it? Or *can* it?

Pasiphae and the Bull

Pasiphae was the wife of King Minos and they lived down on the island of Crete, which is only a short boat ride from the Greek mainland. Now, despite the fact that Pasiphae is married to the King of Crete, she gets struck with one of Cupid's arrows and falls madly in love with a bull—not your regular basketball bouncing "Chicago Bull," mind you—but a real, live, dirt-stomping, horn-bearing, cud-chewing *bull*. Now, if you're King Minos, you see all the pussy you want. After all, you're The King! So I think it's safe to say that if Minos chose Pasiphae as his wife, Pasiphae was no warthog. But beauty that she was, she could not get the bull to give her a second look.

You see, this bull—he's a real stud, too—*literally*! So he certainly didn't have to wander far a field to get his hot little horns on all the "bovine booty" any bull could ever want. Besides, being a bull and not of the human species, the prospect of "Pasiphean pussy" wasn't about to get his big, bull dick hard, no matter how beautiful Pasiphae was or how many times she fluttered through the meadow wearing her skimpiest *peplos*.

Because it was one of cupid's arrows that brought about the whole situation, Minos had no choice but to suck it up and deal with it. Likewise, when Cupid hits you, he hits you hard, so Pasiphae is in deep. So Minos, having grown weary of listening to his wife's constant weeping and wailing about that goddamned bull, goes to Daedalus, who was sort of the handyman around the palace, and begs for his help.

Now, coming up with a way to get the Queen to "hook up" with the bull is not your everyday request—I mean, it's not like unclogging a sink or replacing some broken roof tiles—so old Daedalus is stumped. But being handy and all, he's got an idea and goes to work. Every day, for weeks and weeks, Pasiphae would stop by the shop and ask Icarus what his father was planning, and every day Icarus, who was under strict orders to say nothing (and Icarus *always* obeyed his father's orders), said nothing.

Ta-Da!

Finally, the big day arrives and the whole family breathlessly gathers in the atrium of the palace as Daedalus unveils his work. There, before them on a wheeled platform stood a life-sized replica of a heifer. Carved out of the hollow trunk of a great cypress tree, Daedalus designed the interior to Pasiphae's exact physical measurements. Furthermore, so that the Queen would be the more comfortably accommodated, he fitted out the entire cavity of the torso with a fine grade leather interior. Under its belly, Daedalus showed Pasiphae the trap door through which she would climb inside.

Once inside the heifer, Pasiphae realized that Daedalus had designed the interior to hold her body in a very specific position. As she wriggled inside, her arms slid down into the shoots of the wooden heifer's hollow front legs; likewise, her legs slipped effortlessly down into the broad, empty sockets of each of the heifer's hollow hind quarters. With her body in this position—it reminded her of something she had once heard her husband refer to as the "doggie style"—the Queen found that her cute little Greek ass was snuggly nestled into the cheeks of the hollow rump of the beast. As she lay there, Pasiphae could feel a slight draft wafting right up her cunt, which was all but hanging out of a second trap door Daedalus had cut dead center under the heifer's tail. While the trap door in the belly had been for Pasiphae to enter the heifer—and could close and latch—the hole under the tail had no door, it was open for the bull to enter Pasiphae!

> **Anatomical Note:** Our word "cunt" derives from the Latin noun *cunnus*, and was the word for the female sexual organ used in copulation. If you said "I want your *vagina*" to a Roman girl, she'd probably respond "I don't have one, but I think my brother does."

And Enter He Did!

Daedalus had designed the wooden heifer to the exact specifications necessary for the bull to mount it with Pasiphae inside with her tight little tush tucked up right where it needed to be so that the bull could achieve complete penetration with ease. So, with Pasiphae having "assumed the position," as the saying goes, they wheel the contraption out into the middle of the meadow where the bull grazed. And then they waited…

They didn't have to wait for long. So accurately had Daedalus designed that bogus heifer that it got the attention of the bull almost right away. It wasn't long before the bull came sniffing around. Three times did it circle the heifer and then with a sudden lunge—a lunge that in its ferocity seemed to take everyone by surprise—particularly Minos—the bull flung himself on that wooden heifer's ass with the force of a freight train landing on a rowboat. The bull mounted the heifer and pounded away with such rage and—at the same time, it seemed, passion—mounted and pounded with all the bull that was in him such that King Minos couldn't bring himself to watch any longer.

But averting his eyes didn't spare him the degradation of having to listen to the shrieks and whimpers of his Queen as she took everything that bull with his big bull cock was hammering home—and from the sounds of it, she *liked* it. Even from across that broad meadow, with the Queen shut up inside the wooden heifer and the bull howling and grunting to the high heavens, the King knew the sounds of his Queen's pleasure.

No one could have predicted what was to be the outcome of all this. Evil omens began appearing left and right. The moon shone red as blood. Birds dropped dead from the sky for no apparent reason. And then came the kicker: after a few months had gone by, suddenly the word around the palace is that Pasiphae is "late." The bull had impregnated her. No one knew what to expect, and all they could do was wait. And in the end, it was even more horrible than anyone could have imagined. One thing was for sure: life around the palace would never be the same again.

Congratulations, It's a…Minotaur?

The monster Pasiphae gave birth to had the head of a bull and the body of a man. Someone at the palace gave it a nickname and it stuck: the *Minotauros*, or "Minos' Bull." They tried to raise the thing in the palace, but it had terrible table manners, could never master the knife and fork, growled and howled at the moon—and had, in general, poor personal hygiene. Not to mention those horns of his were wreaking havoc on the upholstery. So Minos goes to Deadalus again, this time he asks him to build some sort of coop or cage—some damn thing—in which to keep the fucking thing locked up and out of sight. They couldn't have this thing running around tearing up the palace any longer.

What Daedalus designed was the famous Labyrinth at Knossos—an underground, intricate maze that led through countless twists and turns to an inner chamber where the beast was kept and cared for. See, the Minotaur wasn't very bright, so there was no danger of his ever finding his way out, and once the palace servants learned their way through the maze, they could easily slip in and out to fill the Minotaur's kibble bowl, make sure it had ample fresh water, and change the litter in its litter box.

As for King Minos and Pasiphae, things were never quite the same between them—like they say, once you "go bovine," you don't come back. So they ended up taking separate bedrooms, as married folk tend to do, and pretty much avoiding each other as best they could. It was a large palace and Crete, after all, is a rather large island, as islands go.

A Menu Fit for a Minotaur

Try finding one! The construction of the Labyrinth solved only part of the problem. As the Minotaur grew it developed a voracious appetite, and they could *not* find *anything* to satisfy it. There were indications that the monster had a certain penchant for a carnal menu, because sometimes they would send in three servants and only two would come back out. But Minos did not have an endless supply of slaves, so they had to find an alternate means of supplying the monster with fresh bodies.

Meanwhile, Minos had become so weary of the situation on Crete that he did what most Kings do when they get bored or frustrated: he started attacking his neighbors. It got him off the island for a while and helped take his mind off the "Minotaur problem." Many of the captured were sent back to Crete as fodder for the Minotaur. But Minos couldn't keep making war forever—more to the point, he couldn't keep *winning* them forever.

Take Athens, for Example

Minos couldn't. Not for lack of trying, though. Out of all of his military ventures, Minos could never manage to breach the defenses of the city. Athens was famous for her "long walls" built during the Peloponnesian War. So he prayed to the gods to send a deadly plague upon the city. They did. Plagues are nasty things, so finally Aegeus, the king of Athens, offered a deal. If Minos would get the gods to call off the plague, he would send an annual tribute of seven virgin boys and seven virgin girls to satisfy Minotaur's unholy appetite. Minos accepts the terms, Athens delivers on the virgins, the Minotaur finally shuts the fuck up, and life on the island is somewhat bearable for Minos again.

Deadalus, on the other hand, was beginning to get worried. Crete had become a wild and wacky place—there was the Minotaur, for one thing, plus—since Minos had returned from Athens—he was starting to get these dark and glowering looks from the King as though the whole mess had been *his* fault, when all he had done was to obey the King's orders So he came up with a scheme for him and his son, Icarus, to escape from the island. Working in secret down in his shop late at night, he fashioned two pairs of wings out of feathers and some wax—wings that he and Icarus could use to fly off the island—two one-way tickets to freedom!

They waited for the day when the wind was favorable, and then took to the sky from the tallest peak on the island. Before taking off, Daedalus warned his son Icarus not to fly too close to the sun, because the heat from the sun would melt the wax and the feathers would fall out and if *that* happened, it would be a real short trip.

Flyboys Will still Be Boys

Icarus was a good boy, and always listened to his father. But once he got up there, in the middle of all that blue sky and fresh air, it really put the zap on his head and he began to have some fun with his new wings, soaring ever higher and higher…

Meanwhile Deadalus, just happy to be off the island, had his attention focused on the mainland and where they might make the best landing. As a result, he was not paying as close attention to Icarus as he should have been. When he finally did look around for the boy, it was too late. Icarus was spiraling downward toward the sea, flapping his featherless arms in useless effort until he slammed into the water. To this day, the area of the Aegean in which Icarus crashed bears his name as the Icarian Sea, and a nearby island was also named Icaria in his honor.

As for the Minotaur, eventually the plague ran its course and Aegeus decided enough was enough, so with the next boatload of virgin boys and girls that he sent to Crete, he also had a hit man named Theseus smuggled aboard, with a contract to take out the Minotaur. But once they reached Crete, Theseus was faced with the problem of the Labyrinth. Even if he could find his way *in*, how was he going to find his way *out*?

Get a Clue, Pal

Theseus didn't have a clue. So he went out and bought one. No, it wasn't a map to the Labyrinth (which, if one existed, would have worked just as well), it was a ball of twine. Which he unwrapped as he worked his way through the many twists and turns of the Labyrinth, thus leaving a trail for him to follow on the way back. Interestingly, it is from this story that we get our word "clue," as it comes directly from the Greek word *clōn* (κλων) which means "ball of string." Without it, Theseus would have been "clueless" as to how to find his way out of the Labyrinth after slaying the Minotaur!

Theseus also had a little help from Ariadne, Minos' daughter, who was also looking for a one-way ticket off the island. So in exchange for her help (she held the end the of the twine as he unraveled it), she got to hitch a ride with him the hell out of there.

Watching your "Dents" and "Odonts"

The Latin root for tooth is *dent*, and in Greek, it is *odont* (οδοντ). We can see a similar relationship in their roots when we compare them, just as with the Latin root for foot (*ped*) and the Greek root (*pod*). The fact that we use both the Greek and the Latin roots with such regularity in our jargon about teeth and feet should tell us something about how important it was for both the Greeks and the Romans to learn all they could about the human body, and that they shared much of their knowledge

One who works on teeth, in general, is a "dentist,' a word built on the Latin root *dent* plus the "occupational suffix" "ist." If your dentist tells you that you need braces to straighten your teeth, he might refer you to an "orthodontist," a word built on the Greek adverb ορθως (say: "or-thōs") meaning "straight,' and οδοντ, the Greek word for "tooth." Not flossing enough? You might need to see a "periodontist," someone who works on the area "around" (περι—say: "peh-ree") your teeth (οδοντ), which would be your gums.

Say Ahh...

By the time people reach the age of about twenty, most have a full set of thirty-two teeth. Just like the other parts of the body, teeth have names as well, and they were given to us by the Romans and the Greeks.

Starting at the rear of the mouth, your "molars" are the teeth with the largest surface in the mouth. The word "molar" comes directly from the Latin word *molar* meaning "millstone," because your molars are the teeth you mainly use to "grind" your food. Most people have twelve molars in their mouths: three upper left three upper right, etc.

Wise Up!

Your third molars, the ones way in back, are referred to as your *dentes sapientiae* or, literally, "teeth of wisdom." They are called this because they are the last to emerge, usually when you are older and therefore considered wiser. Some people's "wisdom teeth" never emerge. They're considered the lucky ones, because when the third molars appear, they often end up crowding the others and therefore have to be removed. This doesn't mean that after you have your wisdom teeth removed you're going to end up more stupid than when you had them in. More than likely, you will just be broke. Dental work can be extremely expensive, so wise up and take care of your teeth!

Beware of Dog!

The three teeth in front of the molars are called, naturally, your "premolars." After them come your "canine" teeth. You only get one of these on either side of your mouth, upper and lower, but because they are the longest and sharpest teeth in your mouth, that's all you really need. The name derives from *canis*, the Latin word for dog, because a dog's "canines" are also the longest teeth in *his* mouth, and they're all *he* needs when it comes to ripping and tearing into flesh.

The only reason a Roman would have kept a dog around the house would have been for protection. Remember, this was before there was anything like an organized "police force" and so it was the responsibility of every man to protect his own stuff. That's why many people still have them today. It is a very common sight when exploring the ruins in Pompeii, for example, to find a *cave canem* mosaic on the floor of the entrance to a house—letting all visitors know: beware of dog! The dog was also the mascot of the Roman army. Dogs, being "pack animals" by nature, were fiercely loyal to their fellow soldiers who fed and cared for them, and alongside whom they marched as well as fought into the thick of battle.

Back to your (Front) Teeth

Your front four teeth are known as your "incisors." The word may come from the Latin verb *incidere*, which means "to cut into" and breaks down to the prefix "in" plus *caedere*, the verb meaning "to cut." When we put the two together, "vowel shortening" causes the diphthong "ae" of *caedere* to change to the "i" of the verb *incidere*. Other etymologists feel that the word is made up of "in" plus the Latin verb *scindere*, meaning "to tear." There's no way to prove it until you bite into your next steak and then you tell me!

Going to the Dentist

Nobody likes to go to the dentist's office—least of all, probably, the dentist himself! I mean, being a dentist had better be your "vocation" because as a "job" it would suck to have to spend your whole day looking to people's mouths.

Like most people, I know I am supposed to visit my dentist twice a year, but like most people I only seem to go when nature calls—and when it comes to dental pain, nature doesn't "call," it "shouts!" So the last time I went to visit the dentist, it was because of a cavity I'd been ignoring in my upper left "second molar"—also known simply as "number two" in dentists' parlance. Now I have an excellent dentist, and for him, I'm sure—and I damn well *hope*—dentistry is his "vocation" because he really seems to have a good time with it. In fact, he appears to be having so much fun, that if he hadn't turned out a dentist, he would have made an excellent stand-up comedian. He even does "impressions"—and not just of my teeth!

Now, because he's going to have to be drilling in there, what happens first is he gets me in that chair and shoots my face so full of Novocain that I can't even tell that I *have* a face let alone a *mouth*!

> **Etymological Note:** Novocain was originally developed in England around 1905 and comes from the Latin adjective *novus* meaning "new" plus the suffix "caine" abstracted from cocaine, a popular (and at the time still legal) pain reliever that was also used by early dentists for its numbing powers. The suffix "aine" is a variant of "ine," a suffix forming nouns and used in the names of chemical elements, such as "chlorine," but it's also used in the names of compound substances such as "cocaine, a compound of the coca leaf plus the suffix "ine."

Seeing Jesus

After he's got the Novocain in me, he hooks me up to the nitrous oxide and then disappears for about twenty minutes while the Novocain takes hold. Now most dentists won't hook you up to the nitrous until after they come back and are ready to get started. If they do put the mask over your nose, just to fuck with you—the bastards—they keep you on pure oxygen until they're ready to start.

Not *my* guy. He hooks me right up to the old "goofy gas" and lets me lie their and hallucinate for a while, which can be very relaxing because usually after about thirty seconds I'm seeing Jesus. By the time my dentist comes back in and gets ready to go to work, I think *he's* Jesus!

First, he fills my mouth with all sorts of irrigation tubes and drains. Then, as he starts drilling away, he begins asking me all sorts of questions! Stuff like, "I wonder how they did all this back in the ancient Roman days, heh-heh..." And of course there's so much hardware and crap in my mouth—not to mention his hands and that goddamn *drill*—that the best I can do is make these gurgling sounds. But this seems to have no effect on my dentist, who goes on to tell me about this trip he's planning to take to Rome this summer and where would I recommend that he stay and what should he see first and where should he eat and should he take a train or...

The drilling just keeps going on and on, chunks of enamel—the hardest substance in the human body, by the way—flying this way and that around my mouth. But by now I'm so gassed up that I'm no longer in my dentist's chair, I'm strapped onto an examination table in a Martian space ship about to be given "the procedure..."

"Oooh, this is a *deep* one," I hear him say over the sound of the drill, which is not the sound of a drill but the whirring of a Martian turbo engine. Then, as though he's expecting to strike oil down there, he presses even deeper with the drill and suddenly I feel something go flying out of my mouth and hit my kneecap! "That ought to do it," the Martian says, and in no time he's got me filled in and straightened out and back on my merry way.

What Has *Teeth* on one end …

…has *tail* on the other. Your teeth actually play a big role in the digestive process. There is a direct relationship between how well your teeth processes food coming into the body through the orifice of the mouth, and the condition of what's left of it when it comes out of that…*other* orifice. In between is something called the "digestive system," which helps make up for what the teeth cannot accomplish—but your teeth are the first line of attack in the digestive process. So if your teeth aren't in good condition, you could end up with a real pain in the ass!

Just a little more Proctalgia

Aside from the seeing your dentist regularly, another medical procedure that most people—men, particularly—ought to keep up with but manage to avoid like the plague is a visit to their friendly neighborhood proctologist. The word "proctologist" comes from the Greek word *proctos* (προκτος) meaning "ass" or "anus," and the suffix "ologist." So, a proctologist is someone who "studies asses"—and we're not talking about everyone's favorite pastime during bikini season, either! There's a word for that, I'm sure, but "proctology" isn't it!

Now watch this: if you take the root *proct* and add it to the root *alg*, meaning "pain," you get the adjective "proctalgic," which means, literally, "having the ability to be a pain in the ass!" The noun would be "proctalgia." Try it, next time you want to tell someone what you *really* think of them or of something they want you to do. I guarantee you they won't have a clue as to what you're talking about and will probably take it as a complement!

The Story
Part One: The Greeks

CHAPTER 10

What's *Your* Story?

Everyone has a story, and most people given the chance will tell you theirs—like it or not. We are a society of storytellers. Because societies are made up of individuals, each with his or her own story, *The Story* of any given society is in many ways an amalgamation of the many stories of the many individuals who make—and who throughout history have made—up that society.

"What a big chariot! He must be compensating for something…"

> **Etymological Note:** "Amalgamation" is a big fancy word generally used in the context of metallurgy—the forging of alloys through the smelting of different types of metals. The ancient Greeks and Romans became very skilled in this craft, and it enabled them to emerge from the dark days of the "Iron Age," survive the crude weapons of the "Bronze Age," and arrive safe and sound at their "Golden Age." But big and fancy as it is, the root of the word "amalgamation" is small and simple enough to find once we break it down into its original elements: *amal · gam · ation*. The first part of the word, "amal" (*am-al*) is of Arabic origin and is the part of the word that has to do with "metals." The suffix ("ation") simply makes the word into a noun. What we're left with is the root of the word, *gam*, from the Greek noun *gamos* (γαμος) meaning "marriage." So, literally, an "amal*gam*ation is a "marriage of metals." I chose this word specifically because it is with a marriage that *The Story* of what we call "Ancient Civilization" begins.

The "cast of characters" we've met so far—Apollo, Cassandra, Achilles, Helen, Atreus, Zeus and Hera—and many others that we've yet to meet—are all players in *The Story*. It's a "creation myth," actually, because *The Story* is the narrative that chronicles the birth of a civilization. Along the way, we'll witness the rise and fall of the Greeks, the destruction of Troy, lots of rape, slaughter, good old fashioned mayhem, and end up with the founding of Rome. We refer to *The Story* as a "myth" because it was passed by mouth from generation to generation long before someone got around to writing it down.

The First Tellers of *The Story*

One of the first people—if not the *first* person—to put stylus to scroll and set *The Story* down in writing was a man called Homer, believed to be the author of the *Iliad* and the *Odyssey*—two *long* narrative poems written sometime around 800 B.C. But because Homer is believed to have been blind, it stands to reason that someone else did the actual writing. Homer marks a significant change in our progression toward *The Story* of Classical Civilization. Up to this point, stories were passed down by mouth (μυθος) and so were considered "myths." As soon as old Homer got his poems set down in writing, he moved us from the spoken word (μυθος)—the raw stuff of mythmaking—to the written word (εποος), the stuff that "epics"—long narrative poems—are made.

We are also especially indebted to three other men, playwrights, who lived about five hundred years after Homer: Aeschylus, Sophocles, and

Euripides—or, as they're officially known among Classisists, "The Big Three." These three men, carrying on in the tradition of Homer—by using many of his characters and their stories—wrote plays whose plots and story lines form the tapestry that would become *The Story*. Unfortunately, of the nearly four hundred plays that "The Big Three" are believed to have written in their lifetime, only thirty-three have survived. These became the raw stuff of what we today refer to as "theatre." But the origins of the Greek theatre can be traced back even farther than Aeschylus, Sophocles, and Euripides—all the way back to some of the earliest traditions of civilized man: the celebration of the harvest.

> **Etymological Note:** During the harvest, the Greek farmers would pile their wheat around in a circular threshing floor and then walk around and around in that area, tossing the wheat up in the air with a rake-like tool called a "winnowing fork," letting the wind blow the chaff away while the heavier kernels of the grain fell to the ground. The round area in which this took place was called the *orchestra* (ορχηστρα), and after all the winnowing of the grain was completed, the farmers would celebrate by dancing and singing in the *orchestra*.

Over the centuries, this custom evolved into a formal, organized public festival that attracted a huge audience. While some just watched, others participated on a regular basis and became known for their particular talents—singing, reciting poetry, plucking the lyre, etc. In other words, what we're talking about is the birth of "theatre."

In the Greek theatre of, say, Euripides' day, the orchestra had become the area where the chorus, who interacted with the players on the stage, sang and danced. It was in the fifth century B.C. that the Greek theatre took the shape that most theatres still have today. In the fifth century B.C., playwrights wrote plays which were performed during the festival of Dionysus, the god of wine, women, and song, and were produced in the Theatre of Dionysus located on the southern slope of the Acropolis in Athens.

The early festivals were elaborate affairs, lasting for days, and the plays were judged and prizes were awarded—for the best play, best performance by an actor in a leading role, etc. The winners were awarded crowns of laurel leaves and finely crafted, hand-made vases, many of which survive today. Perhaps some of the best collections of Greek red and black figure pottery can be found in the Metropolitan Museum of Art in New York City and the British Museum in London.

> **Theatrical Note:** The tradition of awarding actors still goes on today. We have awards for theatrical performances on both the stage and the screen. The award for an outstanding theatrical performance on the stage is called the 'Tony," named after an American actress and producer, Antoinette Perry (1884-1946), who also served as the chairman of the National Theater Council. For performances on the big screen, The Academy of Motion Picture Arts and Sciences awards a ten inch high, gold-plated statuette that today is famously known as the "Oscar"—but it wasn't always that way. First awarded in 1927, the statue didn't have a name and remained nameless until 1931, when Mrs. Margaret Herrick, a librarian at the Academy, casually remarked to a co-worker that the statue resembled her uncle Oscar. By coincidence, the conversation was overheard by a reporter who was working in the library, and the next day, in an L.A. newspaper, a story appeared informing the public that employees of the Academy had affectionately named their famous statuette the "Oscar." And the name stuck.

The *Personae Dramatis*

Because the mythologies of Greece and Rome are so tightly interwoven, you can't tell *The Story* without telling the individual stories of both cultures. We'll do our best to keep things from getting confusing by splitting *The Story* up into two parts: in this chapter, we'll focus on the Greek highlights of *The Story*. In the next chapter, we'll see how *The Story* evolved from the one culture to the next. What's most fascinating is how the two civilizations and their principle players merge so effortlessly in the collective consciousness of modern society. It's not an easy suitcase to unpack.

First of all, the ancient Greeks and Romans were pagans and polytheists, and they shared many of their gods and the stories surrounding them. But because the Romans spoke Latin and the Greeks spoke, well, Greek, most of the main gods and heroes had two names—one Greek and one Roman. For example, if the Greeks were telling the story of a hero who fought at Troy and then took ten years to get home again, they'd be talking about a man named "Odysseus" (Οδυσσευς). If the Romans were sitting around telling the same story, they'd be talking about a man named "Ulysses." They're similar, you can see that. Another instance would be with the Roman hero "Hercules." The Greeks called him "Herakles." Likewise, most gods had a Greek and a Roman name, even though, for the most part, their roles and status within the hierarchy of the gods stayed pretty much the same.

Greek Name	Roman Name	Role
Zeus	Juppiter	King of the gods
Hera	Juno	Wife (and sister) of Zeus
Poseidon	Neptune	Ruler of the Sea
Hades Pluto	Saturn	Ruler of the Underworld
Athena	Minerva	Goddess of Wisdom
Aphrodite	Venus	Goddess of Sex
Ares	Mars	God of War
Artemis	Diana	Virgin Goddess of the Hunt
Hermes	Mercury	Messenger of the Gods
Hephaestus	Vulcan	Blacksmith God of Fire

In the case of a few gods, like Apollo, Dionysus (Bacchus), and some of the minor deities, the Greeks and Romans shared the same names, which makes things a little easier on everybody.

Anatomy of a Story

All stories—and I'm talking about the ones that playwrights used as plots for their plays and the poets of antiquity drew on for material for their narrative poems—have three basic "acts" Or "movements." There's no getting around it. Act One: get your people up a tree; Act Two: shoot at them while they're trapped up in the tree; Act Three: get them down from the tree. There are many variations (boy finds girl, boy loses girl, etc.), but the tri-partite structure—the necessity for a Beginning, a Middle and an End—is as old as storytelling itself.

The other ingredient necessary—no, *mandatory*—in a story is "conflict." No one wants to hear about a guy who wakes up, goes to work, has a great day, and then comes back home. *Booooring*! The first story that was written down, the *Iliad,* begins with a fight, a quarrel over a woman, as we'll see. All the surviving plays of Aeschylus, Sophocles, and Euripides also center around conflict—often resulting in the extreme reversal of fortune of the main character. The great man brought low. No one cares if a mule skinner's life turns to shit, but when the King of Thebes falls from the lofty heights of power and respect to the shame and disgrace of scandal and public humiliation— now *that's* entertainment! But that's *not* what makes it a "tragedy."

The Wedding of Peleus and Thetis

All societies have some form of a creation myth—the "story" of how their world came about. Often these are seen as religious accounts, and this is also true of *The Story* we're talking about. Where these stories begin is often a very murky business. We don't even know how *our* story really begins. Some of us believe that it starts with the "Big Bang" theory (talk about *conflict!*), others with Adam and Eve—who probably shared a few "big bangs" of their own after they ate the apple pie and their landlord evicted them from the garden.

The Greeks and Romans begin their Story with the wedding of Peleus and Thetis. Now, Peleus is a mortal and Thetis is a goddess—a sea nymph, to be exact—and one thing is certain: whenever a mortal man marries a goddess, nothing good ever comes from it. Generally, the lucky groom gets one night of great sex—he was, after all, marrying a goddess—but afterward, he's rendered impotent for the rest of his life. Which is pretty much the kiss of death for any newly married couple. Peleus and Thetis were no exception: they had one child together, the great warrior Achilles, but quarreled over how best to raise him. The marriage ultimately ended in divorce. We'll get back to Achilles later.

The Guest List

Now, in putting together the guest list for the wedding, Peleus naturally invites all of his friends and relatives, and Thetis invites all of hers. But being a goddess, her side of the family is made up of nothing but gods and goddesses, and she invites all of them—except one. A goddess by the name of Eris. Eris (Ερις—say: "eh-riss") had been aptly named using the Greek word for "strife" or "discord," and she cut a dark figure among the Greek gods. Since she wasn't all that pleasant to have around, she was never invited to any of the gods' parties. For starters, she was the daughter of Nyx (νυξ—say: "nooks") which is the Greek noun for "night"— a time in the ancient world when most bad things tended to happen.

Now, Getting back to Nyx, besides being the goddess of night, she is considered to be among the first of the gods to come into existence, born of Chaos (Χαος) at the beginning of time—whenever that was. Along with Eris, she is believed to have brought into the world Thanatos (Θανατος), the god of death, and Geras (Γερας), the god of old age. Not good things. And she accomplished this all by herself, without the help of any man. Talk about "immaculate conception!"

Etymological Note: Often confused with the phrase "Virgin Birth," which Catholics conveniently use to explain away how Mary could have conceived a child without having to undergo the usual erotic ritual—namely *fucking*—the phrase "immaculate conception," first recorded in 1687, was meant to explain how Mary herself sprang from a womb unstained by sperm. The word "immaculate" comes from the Latin prefix "in" which here negates, and the verb *maculare*, which means "to stain."

The Golden Apple

Getting back to the marriage of Peleus and Thetis. Well, this was *one* party Eris was *not* going to be left out of, so she decides to crash the reception. But before she does, she makes a little wedding gift of her own to bring along—a "golden apple," on which she inscribed: "to the most beautiful woman." In ancient Greek, it would have looked like this: τηι καλλιστηι (say: "tey-kal-ist-ay").

So, Eris sneaks into the reception hall and rolls the golden apple across the floor where it comes to a stop near the buffet table. Standing there, helping themselves to some punch and ambrosia are three major goddesses—Hera, Athena, and Aphrodite. Athena sees the apple, picks it up, and says "Look at this beautiful gift someone has made for me!" Hera snatches it out of her hands and says, "What the hell do you mean, 'for you?' Don't you know your ancient Greek? It says 'τηι καλλιστηι,' which is the dative singular of the superlative form of the feminine adjective for 'beautiful,' and that can only mean *me*!" Upon hearing the translation (ancient Greek had always been her weakest subject in school), Aphrodite grabs the apple from Hera and says "Not so fast! Everyone knows *I'm* the most beautiful woman. If *that's* what it says, then this apple must be meant for me!" Suddenly, a catfight erupts among the three goddesses as they begin to wrestle over the apple. They upset the buffet table, with ambrosia and shrimp pâté flying everywhere.

From across the hall, Zeus caught sight of this spectacle and hurried over to break it up. The only way to settle this, he said was to have a contest to see who among them was truly the rightful recipient of the apple. He dispatched Hermes, the swiftest of the gods, to find a judge for what would become the world's first beauty pageant. Hermes goes flying off and soon spots a young man by the name of Paris, tending his flocks on the grassy slopes of Mt. Ida. Mt. Ida is in northern Asia minor, near the city of Troy—which just happened to be his home because his father was Priam, the King of Troy. Hermes appears before Paris, hands him the golden apple, and explains the situation. Zeus wants Paris to do him a little favor. Paris knows *The Rules*, too, and realizes that he is in a no-win situation. What can he do? What Zeus "wants," Zeus "gets."

The World's first Beauty Pageant

So here, now, standing before Paris are Hera, Athena, and Aphrodite—all decked out in their finest *peploi* (πεπλοι—the plural form of πεπλος), and they're looking *hot*. Paris realizes that he is in a real bind. No matter which goddess he chooses, he's bound to piss off the other two.

Hera's Power Play

So while Paris is sweating the situation out, Hera pulls him aside and says "Hey, Paris, you know who *I* am. I'm the *Queen* of the gods! I am the most *powerful* of *all* the goddesses. If you choose *me*, I'll make *you* the most powerful man in the *world*. Kings and their armies will kneel before you! *You* will rule the world!" And Paris thinks: "Well, power is good. I like power. And everybody wants to rule the world, right?"

Athena's Smart Move

Now, while Paris is pondering Hera's offer, Athena pulls him aside and says, "Hey, Paris, you know who *I* am. I'm Athena, the goddess of *wisdom*. If you pick *me*, I'll make you the wisest man on earth. Kings will cross the wine dark sea to seek your council. You'll know what thoughts lie deep in men's hearts and all the secrets of the universe." And Paris thinks to himself, "Wisdom is good. I like wisdom…" He's also starting to realize that maybe this might not be such a bad gig after all—judging this beauty pageant. It's starting to look like there might be something in this for *him*. So he plays along, waiting to see where this will lead.

Aphrodite Drives a "hard" Bargain

While Paris is pondering Athena's offer of wisdom and Hera's promise of power, Aphrodite pulls Paris aside and says "Hey, Paris, you know who *I* am. You know what *I'm* the goddess of. If you pick *me*, I'll give you the most beautiful woman in the world to have as your wife and to do with as you please!"

The Judgment of Paris

Paris was actually already married to a nymph by the name of Oenone, daughter of the River Cebren, but he was also only about eighteen and busting out with hormones. He could not resist Aphrodite's offer. Power? Wisdom? Who cared about those when there's pussy involved?

So, faster than you can say "poontang," he announces Aphrodite as the winner, "the fairest of them all." Aphrodite keeps up her end of the deal, saying, "Okay, her name is Helen, she lives in Sparta," and jots down her address. But what she fails to tell Paris is that Helen, like Paris, is also married—to a man named Menelaus, none other than the *King* of Sparta!

The (Poor) Judgment of Paris

Aphrodite used her power to influence Paris' father, Priam, to send Paris on some embassy to Sparta, unaware of the true purpose of the trip. Conveniently, soon after Paris arrives, Menelaus was called out of town on business leaving Paris and Helen alone. With a little more help from Aphrodite, Helen falls madly in love with Paris and they elope, taking with them a bunch of Menelaus' treasure as they sail back to Troy. It probably wasn't the best move Paris could make, but when you're only about eighteen, what do you expect? Once the two lovers set sail for Troy, there was no turning back.

When Menelaus returned to find his wife had run off with Paris, he is madder than a raped ape! Paris has *fucked* with the *wrong Greek*! Menelaus is not just some *schmo* or *schmuck*—he's the *fucking King of Sparta*—a guy with enough clout to unite all the kings of Greece to support his cause and before you can say "trireme," they've fleeted up and set sail for Troy to settle the score.

> **Etymological Note:** Both *"schmo"* and *"schmuck"* are Yiddish words—a language derived from Middle High German and spoken by East European Jews and their descendants. It is written in the Hebrew alphabet but contains borrowings from Russian, Polish and English. Eventually, English started borrowing them back, and so we get a lot of "Yiddishisms" in English today—many of them obscene or derogatory—but often retaining a jocular tenor. For example, a "*schmo*" (or the variant "*schmoo*") is the Yiddish term for a "stupid," or "foolish," or "boring" person (which actually described Menelaus quite accurately). First recorded around the end of the Second World War, it became popular in The States when the cartoonist Al Capp created an egg-shaped creature he named "Schmoo," for his strip *L'il Abner*. And poor old Schmoo took a lot of abuse. Others feel that *"schmo"* may be a truncated form of *"schmuck,"* which is Yiddish for "penis"—more specifically, it's the term used for the foreskin of the penis that is removed during circumcision.

The Trojan War

As a result of Paris' poor judgment, the Greeks laid siege to the city of Troy for ten years. But Troy was a city whose walls were built by the hands of Poseidon and could not be breached by mortal hands—certainly not a *Greek's* mortal hands. Our primary source for the account of the Trojan War as we have it today is Homer's *Iliad*, which recounts the events of the final year of the war. Although the Greek army was under the leadership of Agamemnon, Menelaus' older brother, the mightiest of the Greek heroes under Agamemnon's command is Achilles. The problem is, Achilles and Agamemnon can't stand each other—*conflict*, remember? To make the situation worse, it was fated by the gods that the Greeks could not take Troy without the aid of Achilles. Even though Agamemnon hates Achilles, because he can't win the war without his help, he has to put up with him. And Achilles, because it is also fated that he must fight and die at Troy, hates Agamemnon because he has to fight all his battles for him. It was a really *fucked-up* situation.

The *Iliad*

In fact, the *Iliad* begins with an argument between Achilles and Agamemnon over a young girl who had been captured during a raid on a temple of Apollo. Although Achilles conducted the raid and got the girl himself, Agamemnon uses his status as King to take her from him. Although Achilles is the greatest of the warriors at Troy, Agamemnon, being King, has greater authority than Achilles. He knew it, and he used it.

Achilles wasn't what you would call a "team player" to begin with and as a result of this insult to his pride, he stalks off and withdraws to his ship and refuses to continue to fight for the Greeks any longer. Nor does he allow any of his Myrmidons, the men under his command, to fight either.

> **Mythological Note:** Because the Myrmidons were so loyal to Achilles—not to mention nearly as fierce on the battlefield as he—the term "myrmidon" is applied to anyone who follows orders, generally without question or scruples.

In the end, Achilles and Hector—the greatest of the Trojan warriors—cross swords on the windy plains of Troy. They *fight*. But I won't spoil the poem for you. It's twenty-*fucking*-four books long, for chrissakes, so if I told you how the fight turned out, slogging through the entire poem would be a long way to go for nothing.

Hubris

Achilles' stubborn defiance of Agamemnon lasts for the entire poem. Even though his fellow Greeks are dying by the hundreds on the battlefield every day because he isn't there to defend them, he still refuses to fight. Even after Agamemnon offers to return the girl, he remains resolute. This is a textbook example of what the Greeks called *hubris* (υβις), a word that is nearly impossible to translate into English except to say that it means having a sense of pride or self-importance that is out of proportion to *any* earthly insult. An inability to compromise no matter what the cost. Greek tragedy is full of characters who are the authors of their own downfall because of their "hubris."

In the end, the Greeks finally defeat the Trojans through trickery—the famous "Trojan Horse." But the Trojan Horse actually does not appear in the *Iliad*. The Iliad ends with the war still in progress and a secret meeting in Achilles' tent between him and Priam. Even though the horse that brings down Troy is part of Greek mythology—Aeschylus, for example, mentions it in his *Agamemnon,* a play about the return of the King—it ends up as part of the Roman half of *The Story*, as told by the Roman poet Vergil, in his poem the *Aeneid*, the "sequel," as it were, to the *Iliad*—and a much easier read. First of all, it's in Latin and not ancient Greek; and second, it's only twelve books long, not twenty-*fucking-* four!

The *Odyssey*

The idea of building the Trojan Horse was the brainchild of a clever Greek—known for his cleverness—a hero named Odysseus. Odysseus was the king of Ithaca—an island off the west coast of the Greek mainland and a *long* way from Troy. After the war, he—as well as many of the other heroes who fought there and survived—now have to make their way back home. Not all of them would survive the journey—and many who *did* weren't exactly greeted with open arms upon their return.

Honey, I'm Home!

Agamemnon, for example, gets butchered in the bathtub by his wife Clytemnestra the very night he arrived home. But let's not be too hard on old Clytemnestra. She had her reasons—one of which was that when Agamemnon arrives at the palace, he's got *Cassandra* with him in his chariot as a "war prize!" Mistake number *one*. Not believing Cassandra's prophecy about what awaited him when he got home? Mistake number *two*. Getting into the tub? *Definitely* mistake number *three*.

The *Odyssey* is another *long* narrative poem attributed to Homer that chronicles the adventures of the hero Odysseus on his journey home. It is from his name, obviously, that we derive our word "odyssey" for a long journey. But the *Odyssey* was only one of a series of "homecoming" poems written by Homer and by other poets chronicling the adventures of heroes making their way home after fighting at Troy. Sadly, only one of these survives: Homer's *Odyssey*.

> **Etymological Note:** The Greek word for a poem about a hero's journey home—a "homecoming poem"—is *nostos* (νοστος—say: "noh-stos") Now, watch what happens when we take the root *nost* and splice it onto *alg*, the root of the Greek word for "pain" (αλγος). We get the word "nostalgia." Nostalgia is a very specific kind of pain you should technically feel only at homecomings. We do not use it to describe how you might feel when you get home from work after a long, hard day and maybe your feet ache or your back hurts. Rather, it is used more metaphorically, to describe that feeling you get deep down when you return to a place you maybe grew up in, but haven't seen in a long, long time.

You Can't Go Home Again

Not the way you left, anyway. Greece never really recovered from the Trojan War. They *won* the war, sure, but the victory came at such a price that it was, in every way a classic example of a "Pyrrhic Victory"—nearly a thousand years before the real, actual "Pyrrhic Victory" even took place (see historical note below). The enormous loss of Greek lives, the destruction of Troy—one of the most famous and celebrated cities of the ancient world—all because of the hubris brought on by the abduction of a single *woman*!

For this reason, the Trojan War is an example of "hubris" in the extreme. They never lived it down. It haunted their reputation and preoccupied much of their imagination, as witnessed by their literature and art. In a sense, the "hubris" of the Trojan War put a target on the back of the entire Greek society and everyone who would lead it. It brought them into conflict with the Persians and the Macedonians, until they were finally conquered by the Romans.

> **Historical Note:** Pyrrhus held the throne of Epirus, a territory in northern Greece around 306 B.C. In the year 280, he attacked Rome—he even brought elephants! There were two main battles: one at Heraclea, the other at Asculum in southern Italy. King Pyrrhus was victorious in both encounters, but by the time the second battle was over, he had suffered such heavy losses that—despite the fact that he twice drove the Roman army from the field—he returned home with his army in such shambles that he was said to have remarked "One more victory like that and I'm outta business!"

The Story
Part Two: The Romans

The Fall of Troy

When Homer's *Iliad* ends, the war is still far from over, or so it seemed. But the Greeks, who have encircled the city and are attempting to starve the population into surrendering, are growing weary. They'd come to realize that once Priam, the King of Troy, received the absconded Helen into his city, he must have known that the Greeks would be coming for her sooner or later. Given the amount of time it would take Agamemnon to muster the Greek forces—not to mention cross the Aegean Sea by sail and oar—he would have had plenty of time to stockpile enough provisions to outlast a long, drawn out siege.

But there was still a way. The walls of Troy were built by Poseidon— no getting around that—but because he built them for the Trojans, the *Trojans* could dismantle their walls if *they* wanted to. The question was: *how to make them want to?*

The Trojan Horse

It was the cunning, wily old Odysseus who came up with the idea of how to get the Trojans to dismantle their own walls. One night he had the Greek army build a huge horse from wood collected from the slopes of nearby Mt. Ida—a hollow horse that he designed to hold a small contingent of about thirty of his fiercest, most trustworthy warriors. Then, with the men having been installed within the hollow belly of the wooden horse, the Greeks roll the horse right up to the front of the city gates, then board their ships and sail to Tenedos, an island just off the coast, where they hide in a bay behind the island—just out of sight of the mainland.

The Plan

Now, when Odysseus was drawing up the blueprints for the horse, the first thing he did was measure the gates of the city, and then made the horse a few feet wider on either side, so that when the Trojans would try to bring the horse in through their gates, it would *not…quite…fit* and they would be forced to dismantle part of the walls of their city to make way for the horse to enter. That would be when the rest of the Greeks, hiding off Tenedos, would close in and make their move.

Wake-Up Call

When the Trojans wake up the next morning, they're shocked to find the beach deserted—the Greeks and their ships are gone! In their place, standing before their very gates, is this enormous wooden horse. Its head towering over the walls of the city, as if peering inside.

No one knows what to do. Some think it is a trick, that it should be put to the torch. Others are convinced that the Greeks have given up the siege and returned to Greece having left behind the great wooden horse as an offering to the god Poseidon. See, because Poseidon was a patron deity of Troy (he built their *walls*, for chrissakes!), and because the horse was sacred to Poseidon, many believe the horse should be welcomed into the city, else they might risk offending the god. It's a split decision until…

…Cassandra (remember her?) decides to put her two drachma in. She sees the horse and gets it right away, so she comes running down from the walls shouting "No! No! No! Whatever you do, do *not* bring the horse into the city! It is a *trap*!" Now, remember Cassandra's little run in with Apollo? Because she had tricked her way out of having to eat his "tube steak," she was doomed always to know the future, but to be disbelieved whenever she tried to share it with anyone. So, thanks to Cassandra, the horse comes into the city. The irony of all this, of course, is that Apollo was another one of the patron deities of Troy, yet it was Apollo who cursed Cassandra, and it was Cassandra's curse in turn that ends up bringing Troy down. Greek and Roman mythology is full of such irony.

> **Literary Note:** It is also around this point in the story that Laocoön, the high priest of the city, when he saw the horse being dragged into the city, came running down from the citadel of Troy and said: "Whatever it is, I fear Greeks even when they bear gifts." He did not say "Beware Greeks bearing gifts." This is so often misquoted that I feel it necessary to clear it up here. The line, as Vergil wrote it, reads *Quidquid id est* ("Whatever it is"), *timeo Danaos et dona ferentis* ("I fear Greeks, even when bearing gifts.") Vergil is very clear here. The verb *timere* means "to fear." Had he meant to say "beware Greeks...etc.," he would have used the verb *cavere*, a perfectly good Latin verb that means "to beware." So if you're going to quote the Classics, at least get it right.

The *Aeneid*

This is pretty much where Vergil's poem, the *Aeneid*—a poem about Aeneas, a prince of Troy who managed to escape the city's destruction and go on to found Rome—picks up. After the horse is brought into the city, the Trojans throw a huge bash to celebrate the end of ten years of siege and warfare. Much vino flowed and by midnight, the Trojan revelers were passing out left and right, while silently, darkly amidst them stands the great wooden horse in the center of the city, its hollow belly stuffed full of heavily armed Greek warriors, waiting for their opportunity to pounce.

It came soon enough. With the last of the drunken Trojans nodding off, a small hatch in the underside of the horse silently swings open, and out into the dark Asian night steals Odysseus and his men. Their first course of action is to mount the citadel of the city and by waving torches, signal to the Greek fleet that the city is wide open and theirs for the taking. While the ships raise sail and man the oars in their haste to make it back to the beach, Odysseus and his warriors go on a bloody rampage throughout the city, killing every Trojan—man, woman, and child—that they could lay their hands on.

Mopping Up

The Greek Navy returns to find the city wide open, and in short order, they murder the whole lot of them and burn the city to the ground. In the final, desperate hours of the conflagration, one of the princes of Troy, a young man by the name of Aeneas, manages to escape with a small group of Trojan refugees. In the confusion, he loses track of his wife, Creusa, and only manages to rescue his father, Anchises, and his infant son, Ascanius. Through an underground passage, they make it to the shore, board what few ships they can find and get the heck out of there.

Next stop, Carthage

After fleeing Troy, Aeneas's fleet is destroyed in a storm just off the coast of Carthage. And he and his men are rescued by the Carthaginians. Now, at this point in time, Carthage was a city still under construction and was ruled by a young queen named Dido. Dido was originally from Tyre where here husband, Sychaeus, had been murdered. From there, Dido and her sister, Anna, escaped to the northern coast of Africa. There they were granted asylum by the local King, Iarbas, as well as given land to build a city. In this way, Iarbas hoped to woo Dido into marriage.

Dido Infelix

Dido is perhaps one of the most tragic figures in all of ancient literature. When Aeneas arrives at Carthage, he is taken in by Dido, who, naturally, falls immediately in love with him. She's helped along in this, not by the meddling Aphrodite (who was so instrumental in helping Paris and Helen hook up), but by her Roman counterpart, Venus—remember, we're into the Roman part of *The Story* now, so we're going to have to start using all the Roman names for the gods and goddesses, instead of the Greek ones. If you get confused, just refer to the chart in the previous chapter.

Now, all throughout the *Aeneid*, the primary epithet Vergil uses of Dido is the Latin adjective *infelix*. It is a combination of the prefix "in," which here negates, and *felix*, an adjective which on one level means "happy,' or "lucky." But the root of *felix* is our old friend *fa*. The adjective literally means to "suckle." It comes to mean "happy" or "lucky" because, as we have already seen and discussed, the primary role of a woman in society was to produce offspring. So if you're "suckling," then you've obviously got something to suckle—i.e., a child—thus making you *felix*.

The Latin word for woman is *femina* or *mulier*, so if you were one of these who was unable to have children, whose womb was barren, you were labeled a *mulier* or *femina infelix*—a label which was the kiss of death for any woman. Most translators of the *Aeneid* interpret the phrase *Dido infelix* as simply, "unhappy Dido." But the implication of the epithet is much more personal and telling about her.

This is why Dido fell immediately in love with Aeneas. She was young, a widow, and childless (with the implication of the epithet *infelix* suggesting that she would always remain childless). Likewise, Aeneas is a widower, but he has something Dido does not have and desperately wants—a *son*! In Aeneas are all of Dido's prayers answered and problems solved. An instant family! A queen needs a king, and a *mulier infelix* needs something to suckle.

> **Etymological Note:** The Latin word for "cat, *feles*, is also based on the Latin and Greek roots *fa/fe*, because cats are known to produce large litters and suckle their young at their teats. Most women in ancient Rome probably wished they had been born cats! That's why "Felix the Cat" is always "happy" (as well as redundant!). It is also from this same root that we get the word "fellatio," which means, literally, "to suck someone off." The more common expression is "blow job," but how you get from "blow" to "suck"—which are as different as, say, "give" and "take"—has yet to be explained—or demonstrated, for that matter—to the author's satisfaction. But I did manage to track down the first recorded usage of the verb "to blow" with respect to the act of "cocksucking." In the October 12th 1933 edition of the American tabloid *Brevities*—self-proclaimed "America's First National Tabloid Weekly"—ran the heading "Sexy sailors blow! Bawdy boys run riot on high seas as fags stir emotions of rollicking rovers!" Then, in 1941, G. Legman, in G. W. Henry's *Sex Variants*, defined "blow" as "to fellate or cunnulingue, the object being the person and not the genital organ." In 1959, William H. Burroughs perhaps put it as plainly as you can in his famous work, *Naked Lunch*: "Darling, I want to blow you."

Italia or Bust

Aeneas tells the story of the last hours of the fall of Troy to Dido and her court during a banquet in the palace. It's during the banquet—as she listened to all the heroic efforts of Aeneas and his comrades as they tried in vain to save Troy in its final hours—that she falls deeply in love with him.

Aeneas goes on: as he fled from Troy and wandered the high seas he received a series of visions that informed him that it was he who had been saved from the flames of Troy in order to start a new race. It was his *destiny* to go on and found a new city and home for a future race of

Trojans and that it would be in a place called *Italia*. All he had to do then was *find* it! For two whole books of the poem, Aeneas tells of his escape from the city and his wandering around the sea looking for this place called *Italia*.

Now, Aeneas and his men have to remain in Carthage only long enough to repair their ships, but during this time Dido's love for Aeneas continues to grow deeper and deeper. During his recounting of the fall of Troy, he made it perfectly clear, however, that as soon as his ships were ready, he was going to have to leave. He had something waiting for him called a "destiny" and you can't keep something like "destiny" waiting—you can *try*, but if you do, it has a way of finding *you*. But Dido, being in the throes of deep love, heard only what she wanted to hear. While they're waiting for the ships to be repaired, Aeneas and Dido spend a lot of time together, take long walks in the moonlight—like that. Then, one day, they're out hunting in the woods when a terrible thunder storm separates them from the rest of the hunting party. Together, they take refuge in a cave. The storm is a whopper. So in order to help pass the time, Aeneas shows Dido his sword and demonstrates a little "swordsmanship" for her. It was the wrong thing for Aeneas to do, but what good's a sword if you can't whip it out every now and then.

The day finally arrives—as it always does—when the ships are repaired, the wind is favorable, and it's time for Aeneas and his crew to leave. When Aeneas goes to inform Dido of this, she doesn't take the news very well. She reminds him of what they did in the cave, and asks how he could leave her now after *that*? Didn't that mean *anything*? Aeneas did his best to play it off—what else *could* he do? He promised he'd contact her just as soon as he got to wherever the hell he was going. He even left her his sword as a keepsake of their "time together" in the cave. But in the end, Dido still ends up watching through her tears as Aeneas pulls out of her snug harbor for the last time. If the metaphors aren't obvious enough, Vergil has Dido end her life by throwing herself upon Aeneas' sword.

Italia at Last!

After leaving Carthage, Aeneas finally reaches Italia. But it is not he who founds the city Rome nor was it his son, Ascanius. Aeneas pulls his ships ashore at a place called Latium, a region of Italia named after its king, Latinus. Thus it is from King Latinus, and the region of Latium in which he ruled, that the word "Latin" derives. Aeneas establishes an alliance with Latinus by marrying his daughter Lavinia, but our sources are not reliable enough to know if it is one of Aeneas' descendants or not who finally does found the city of Rome. And in the end, it really doesn't matter because all of this is μυθος.

Taking the "Scholarly" Approach

When trying to tell the story of Rome, it's hard to distinguish between history and myth, especially in the very early days—let alone put a *date* on anything. Most scholars assign 753 B.C. as the date for the founding of the city and attribute its founding to Romulus and Remus, the bastard sons of Mars, the Roman god of war (see below).

It's a good thing we know now that being a "scholar" has nothing to do with being smart or anything like that, it just means you have a lot of free time on your hands. People who believe that real cities can be founded by a man whose father was the God of War maybe have too much free time on their hands!

Romulus and Remus

As the story goes, Mars decides to take a little outing and comes down to earth, where he rapes a young girl by the name of Rhea Silvia. Her father, Numitor, had wanted her to remain a virgin—to be one of the first Vestal Virgins—but Mars "fucked" all that up. She was so ashamed of her resulting pregnancy that after having given birth to the twin boys, Romulus and Remus, she placed them in a wicker basket and floated it down the Tiber River, where it got caught up in some reeds by the Tiber Island, and the two infants were rescued by a she-wolf. Eventually, a shepherd by the name of Faustulus came along and raised the two boys.

The Seven Hills of Rome

Rome is known as the "City of the Seven Hills." These are the Aventine, Palatine, Capitoline, Caelian, Esquiline, Quirinal and Viminal. Once Romulus and Remus had grown up, naturally there arose the question of who was going to be the ruler of the new city. Because the two brothers were twins, it was a complete toss-up as to who would eventually become King. The two brothers quarreled, and Remus took up a position on the Aventine Hill, while Romulus chose the Palatine. Each brother waited while their followers chose sides.

While this was going on, Remus went to work fortifying his position by building a wall around the Aventine hill. Romulus, on the other hand, took up a furrowing plow and plowed a shallow trench around the perimeter of the hill. One day Remus walked over from the Aventine to the Palatine and looked down at the little trench and, laughing, said "How is that meager little trench going to defend your city?" To which Romulus, as legend has it, responded, "It is a *magic* wall. He who crosses it without permission immediately dies."

Leap of Faith

Romulus and Remus might have been twins, but in several key areas—cleverness being one of them, intelligence being another—they were hardly equals. It was as if on the day they were handing out "brains," Remus thought they said "trains," and asked for a "small set." So Remus leaps across the furrow and lands on the other side. Laughing, he says "Ho! Ho! Ho! Look at *me*, little brother! Your 'magic wall' seems to have failed you! I'm not *dead*!" To which Romulus replied, "Oh, yes you are!" and drew his sword and slew him on the spot. Not many people fucked with Romulus after that. In fact, they thought the way he duped old Remus was so slick, they named the city after him!

There are many versions of the story of the founding of Rome, and the details surrounding the murder of Remus by Romulus vary widely, and even our sources, what few we have, are of little use because we're so far back in the mists of time (otherwise known as "pre-history") that historical sources aren't worth the papyrus they're printed on. But what *is* important to take away from all this, is that at the very heart of *The Story* of Rome would always lie the crime of fratricide.

The Tiber Island

The various myths about Romulus and Remus aside, archaeologists and historians agree that the factual reason Rome grew up on the site that it did was the particular topography of the region. The area of the seven hills lies adjacent to a bend in the Tiber River where the river's strong current is broken by an island. It is the only island in the entire river and the fact that it breaks the current makes crossing the river easiest at the island's southern tip.

The Mediterranean Sea, partly because it is essentially a large lake—its only outlet being the narrow opening through the Straights of Gibraltar—has a very high saline content. It is very salty. If you've ever gone for a dip in the Mediterranean, you'd notice that your body has much more buoyancy than, say, if you were to go swimming off the coast of Long Island or Laguna Beach.

Pass the Salt

Where the Tiber Island drains out into the Mediterranean, the strong currents along the shore allow salt pans to form along the northern shore of the mouth of the river. Now, there's a funny thing about us humans, and that is that our bodies require salt. The human body is composed of between sixty to eighty percent water, and the level of sodium in that water is nearly the same percentage as that of the ocean. Maybe this is because life first began in the ocean billions of years ago, but whatever the reason, salt is a necessary ingredient in the human body. It is also a disinfectant and a very good preservative if you're looking to cure meat, or fish. It also makes really bland food taste much better!

The Great Salt Migration

Three or four times a year, people living in the foothills of the Apennine mountain range that runs like a spine down the center of the Italian peninsula journey down to the Tiber Island, cross at the southern tip of the island (where the confluence of the two branches of the river created by the Tiber Island forms eddies and swirls that break the current) and construct a crude bridge or some sort of makeshift rope-tow crossing system.

Meanwhile, up on the Palatine hill, watching all of this going on are Romulus and his crew. Now, being true native Italians, the first thing that crosses their minds is: "How can we get in on the action?" Romulus gets an idea, and the next time one of these tribes of mountain people come wandering down to cross at the southern tip of the island, they find waiting for them a bridge that Romulus and his men had built. "It's up to you," says Romulus, "you can go ahead and take all day to rig up your rickety raft rig of yours, or you can simply use our bridge and pay us with some salt on your way back."

> **Etymological Note:** The root of the Latin word for salt is *sal*, and because it was with salt that these mountain people paid to cross the bridge, it is the root of our word "salary."

Economics 101

They say a good contract is one in which both sides gain something and give something up. The mountain people no longer had to worry about crossing the river, but now they had to supply the Romans with salt. The Romans no longer had to haul their own salt, but now they had a bridge to maintain. So they shook on it, and with that handshake, the economy of what would become the Roman Empire took its first baby steps.

Building Bridges

Now this first bridge at the base of the Tiber Island was made of wood, constructed long before the Romans invented concrete and became master builders with stone. So it was obviously very susceptible to fire, as well as floods and just daily wear and tear. Because this bridge was the basis of Rome's budding economy, its maintenance was taken very seriously and was entrusted only to those whom the early rulers held in the highest confidence.

The official title for this honored position was *pontifex*. The word derives from the Latin root for bridge (*pont*) and the by now familiar root *fact*, from the verb *facere*, "to make" or "build." When we combine these elements, the "a" in *fact* changes through "vowel shortening" to an "e," and the consonantal sound produced by the "ct" changes to the sound "x," giving us "pontifex," which means, literally, "bridge builder." The chief "bridge builder," that is, the magistrate who oversaw the building and maintenance of the first bridges in Rome was called the *Pontifex Maximus*.

The ancient Romans were a very superstitious society, so whenever anything bad happened, it was because a god was angry with them; likewise, whenever good fortune came their way, it was because some god or gods approved of what they had done. If the bridge was struck by lightening, it could only be because they had in some way offended

Jupiter, who hurled the lightening bolt. If the bridge was washed away by the floodwaters of the Tiber when they rose suddenly in the spring thaw, they had offended the god of the Tiber, etc.

For reasons such as these, the early "bridge builders" (plural: *pontifices*) were also men who were expected to be able to communicate with the gods and understand the portents and omens sent by them. It was for this reason that very early on the title of *Pontifex* became a religious title, and the *Pontifex Maximus* was one of the most important and revered religious figures among the many priesthoods in their religion.

As time went on and the Romans began to expand and conquer—first Italy, then the rest of the known world—their economy no longer depended on the maintenance of bridges and bags of salt. By the middle of the first century B.C., Rome was a city with over a dozen bridges and was the commodities exchange capital of the known world. So the role of the *Pontifex Maximus* lost its connection with bridge building entirely and ultimately became the name of the chief religious priesthood in all of Rome.

Historical Note: The Latin word *pontifex* is where we get our word "pontiff," meaning "high priest." While the verb "to pontificate," referring specifically to the Papal activities of the Pope, was first recorded around 1425, "pontiff" was used to refer to the Pope until 1677—although you still here it now and then even today. In ancient Rome, when you were elected *Pontifex Maximus*, you held that position for life. This, too, is another Papal tradition that goes back to the original office of the *Pontifex Maximus*. When you are elected Pope—just as when you were elected *Pontifex Maximus*—you held that office for life. Julius Caesar, for example, was elected *Pontifex Maximus* and remained *Pontifex Maximus* until his murder on the Ides of March, 44 B.C.

How Words Change!

No "Bad" Words

There is no such thing as a "bad" word. I tell this to all my students at the beginning of each semester. How could there be? To teach a class on the history of words and tell my students that we cannot discuss the word "fuck," or "cunt," or "poontang," would be like attempting to teach a course on European history, but informing the class that we're not going to discuss, say, Hitler or Stalin—or even Julius Caesar for that matter—because they killed a bunch of people and so were "bad" men. Now *there's* a course that would be over before it even began! Furthermore, to say that there are "bad" words would then mean by implication that there are "good" words. And what might *they* be? And who decides these things? Once you go down *that* road, there's no end to it—and there's no turning back.

History 101

No one would dispute the fact that Alexander the Great, for example, also killed a bunch of people—even murdered some of his most trusted "friends" just to advance his own ruthless, determined ambition. But the job of an historian is not to judge whether Alexander the Great, or Julius Caesar, or Hitler—or any of the other individuals who make up what we call "history"—were "good" men or "bad" men. The job of a historian is to study these people without moralizing so we can understand them, as a scientist would study, say, a cancer cell. Cancer has killed more people than Hitler, Stalin and Julius Caesar combined—but think how ridiculous it would sound if scientists refused to study such a disease because it had killed millions of people and so was "bad." Looking at the world through the eyes of an objective historian, it is irrelevant whether or not Caesar killed more Gauls than Hitler did Jews (and he might well have!)—both men are a part of the history of our race, just as "poontang" and "cunt" are part of the history of our language—and as scientific specimens, they must be treated in the same objective way.

Keep in mind that a word is simply the product of a series of sounds we emit through our mouths and to which, over the course of hundreds of centuries, we have assigned a "meaning." What is interesting is that the meanings we have assigned to these sounds are, and have been, constantly changing. How and why they change is as much a theoretical phenomenon as the theory of the evolution of our species itself—and the two are inextricably linked.

We have established a scientific approach to this business of etymology in this book, and we're going to stick with it. As we study words, we must continually remind ourselves that we are scientists: morally detached from the focus of our study and so able to approach it without emotion. We break these words down into their original elements and draw conclusions based on our observations. But before we can do that, we must "check our prejudices at the door."

> Etymological Note: Our word "history" comes from the Latin noun historia, meaning a "narrative account," a "story," if you will. Like many Latin words, the noun historia is a direct transliteration of the Greek noun historia (ιστωρια), which means something "known" or "learned through inquiry." Because the root of the Greek word ιστωρια (historia) is the Greek noun istor (ιστωρ) which, ironically, was their word for "judge," "historians" are "judges," just not moral ones. The word "history" first appears around 1393 in the Old French form historie, and we take it from there. Although the "judgments" that historians make are supposed to be objective, it was Richard M. Nixon who said "The judgment of history depends upon those who write it."—but, in Nixon's case at least, one must always consider the source!

How Words Change

Words change their meaning in countless ways, but all of them can be reduced to two main processes: 1) naturally—i.e. simply through practice, custom, tradition, convention, habit, and usage of a word over time; and 2) artificially—i.e. on purpose, by the deliberate, intentional choice of an individual or group of individuals who have an agenda and manipulate words to suit that agenda. Either way, words are ever-evolving, ever-changing, continually adapting to their environment—an environment that is also in a constant state of flux itself. Are you dizzy yet?

Back to *The Story* for a Moment

In the previous two chapters, while explaining *The Story* of the ancient world as the ancients understood it, we discussed a lot of words that began as the first vocabulary of the ancient Greek theatre. This was necessary first of all because the Greeks invented the art form of public dramatic performance; and second, because they used it as a vehicle for conveying different parts and viewpoints of *The Story*—at least the *Greek* side of it—which, of course, was the only side of it they knew. It began with the theft of Helen, culminated with the Trojan War, and ended slowly and painfully with the Greeks condemned to live under the cloud of the "hubris" that they brought upon themselves because of that war and that ultimately got the better of them. The Roman poet Vergil, through the telling of the story of Aeneas' escape from burning Troy and his ultimate landing in Italy, brought *The Story* full circle to a new beginning in a new land. These various aspects of *The Story* became the first material of the early stage—both Greek and, later, Roman—and the characters were, of course, portrayed by actors.

Change over Time

As we discussed in Chapter Ten, the Greek word for "actor" is *hypokrites* (υποκριτης). It is made up of the prefix "hypo" meaning "under" and *crites* (κριτης—say: "cree-tace"), which is another Greek word for judge, and is where we get our word "critic." The actors who participated in these plays were judged and awarded prizes based on their performances—and so for this reason were literally "under the scrutiny of judges"—thus they were called *hypokrites*. Even though the word "hypocrite" is simply the Greek word for "actor," over time—and certainly by the 13th century—the term acquired some heavy social baggage that it still lugs around today. In the Greek world of the 5th century B.C., the term *hypokrites* carried *no* baggage yet, it had no pejorative connotation whatsoever—it was simply the label of what was actually a highly respected profession. Pretending you're someone else, saying great things that are mere fiction, is an art form when you're doing it on the stage, where such behavior belongs, where it is expected—*rewarded*, even. But if you behave that way on the street, in daily life, when you're not on the stage, then it's no longer called an art form (at least not a legitimate one)—in that case it's called "being full of shit," a hypocrite.

Etymological Note: The actors who performed on stage wore masks. These came to be known by the Latin term *persona*. Contrary to popular belief, the primary intention of these masks was not to make the actor *look* like the character he was portraying, rather they had a much more practical use. The masks were made out of terra cotta (fired clay), and around the opening of the mouth, they would build up the clay and fashion it into a short, cone-shaped device that served as a sort of mini megaphone to help project the actor's voice. Even an extra three or four inches of build-up around the mouth was enough to enhance the actor's voice immensely. Try it yourself. Start talking normally, and as you're talking, bring your two hands together and "cup" them around your mouth. You, and anyone else in the room, will be able to hear a marked difference in the volume, tone, and focus of the sound. Because this was the purpose of the masks, they named them accordingly. The word "persona" can be broken down into two elements: the prefix "per," meaning "through," and the root *sona*, which comes from the Latin verb *sonare*, which means "to make noise, produce sound." So the word "persona" literally means something "through which sound passes." Think about it, if you're going to do an "impersonation" of someone, you had better make sure you sound like him, right?

The word "hypocrite" is a good example of how a word changes the natural way—over time, through a blurring of its elements. It is a natural process, the substitution of different uses of its original elements. There is a connection there that can be traced back through the elements of the word without losing sight of their original meaning. An "actor" is by very nature a "liar" in that he makes his living saying things that aren't true—at least with respect to him. It's when he starts doing his "acting" where he shouldn't be doing it—in real life—that the trouble begins.

This is different than the way a word has its meaning changed by someone whose intention is deliberately to misuse a word for his own personal agenda without any regard to what the original elements of that word are. Don't think it doesn't happen—it happens every day, it always *has*, and it always *will*. Take, for example, the word "apple."

Not Another Apple!

Yes, *another* apple! Only unlike the "golden apple of discord" that Eris rolled into the wedding reception of Peleus and Thetis that set *The Story* into motion, the apple we're talking about now is neither golden, nor part of a mythological tale. It is a *red* apple—and as *real* as it is red.

Up until the time when white-skinned Europeans began their great migration across the Atlantic to the continent of America, beginning in the 16th and 17th centuries, an apple was just a piece of fruit. For the first century of this migration, the native American Indians who called this land their home fiercely resisted what they saw as an invasion—which is exactly what it was. But after decades of fighting and bloodshed, many native American Indians eventually realized that Paleface was here to stay—so it was time to go to plan "B."

If You Can't Beat 'Em...

Join 'em, right? Which was exactly how some Native Americans began to see things, and so they lay down their tomahawks and put away their war paint and began to try to assimilate themselves into the white culture. This may have been the smart move, but it was not a point of view shared by all Native American Indians, and the hard core "dead enders," like Geronimo, Sitting Bull and Cochise, who were never going to give in or give up and who were determined to go down fighting, referred to their fellow natives who would rather switch than fight as "apples"—a derogatory term chosen because an apple is red on the outside and white on the inside. Obviously, they didn't use *our* word for "apple" because they didn't speak *our* language—they spoke *their own* languages: the Iroquois must have had their own word for "apple," which was probably different from that of the Navajo or Sioux or Apache. But the metaphor of the apple was what was important. Even though for many years the white skinned European settlers viewed all Indians as savages, as an inferior race, they would rather have them switch than have to keep fighting them. But many Indians viewed their fellow braves who adopted the white man's ways as the lowest form of cowardice and betrayal—what we could call "selling out." They were seen as traitors to their race. They were called "apples."

Watch Out for Labels

This all sounds like such schoolyard "kid stuff," doesn't it? But there is nothing "silly" about putting labels on people. We do it without even thinking twice about it. Students call their professors "Doctor" without knowing why. In your second year in college, they label you a "sophomore," yet most students have no idea what that word means. It's hardly a complement. The word "sophomore" is a combination of the Greek adjective *sophos* (σοφος—say: "soh-foss"), whose root is *soph* and means "wise" and the Greek adjective *moros* (μωρος—say: "mow-ross"), whose root is *mor* and means "stupid" or "dull." It's where we get the word "moron." So a "sophomore" is, literally, a "wise moron." I'm surprised the Political Correctness Police haven't gotten hold of that one yet!

But given time, I'm sure they will. As it is, today we don't have a "chairman" anymore, we have a *chair "person."* We no longer make *snowmen*, we make *snowpeople*. I wonder when they are going to get around to the word pen*man*ship? At the University of Ontario, female professors objected to teaching "seminars" because the root of the word is the Latin noun *semen*, which means "seed." They considered the term sexist, because it is the man who produces the semen. So they coined a new term to replace the term "seminar." What they came up with was the term "ovarium," based on the *female* reproductive equipment. They no longer taught a "seminar," they taught an "ovarium" (plural: "ovaria"). True story.

Jumbo Shrimp

The word "sophomore" is also an example of an "oxymoron," which comes from the Greek adjective *oxus* (οξυς—say: "ox-sus"), whose root, when transliterated is *oxy*, and means "sharp" and the root *mor*, which, as we saw just above, means "dull." So an "oxymoron" is a "sharp dull" thing. The two terms contradict one another and that's exactly what an oxymoron is: a word or phrase that contradicts itself. Classic examples are "jumbo shrimp" and the old standby: "military intelligence." There are many, many more. If you think about it, the term "atomic energy" is an oxymoron because the only way energy can be released from the atom, is by splitting it. The word "atom," as we discussed earlier, is based on the Greek root *tom* meaning "to cut" and the "alpha privative" which negates the root. Until we get that "alpha privative" off the front of the word, we literally cannot release any energy from an "atom" at all.

The Cookie Monster

The apple, because of its "color scheme," was chosen by the Indians as a metaphor for any "red man" trying to fit into the "white man's" culture. Some centuries later, the exact same thing would happen again, believe it or not. Only this time, it was a word used metaphoricaly to stigmatize a "black man" who was perceived by fellow African

Americans men as trying to fit into the "white man's" culture. And the word was *"Oreo."* A *cookie*! Can the world get any weirder than this?

> **Etymological Note:** The word "cookie" derives most directly from the Dutch word *koekje*, the diminutive form of *koek*, which means "cake." Our word "kitchen" also shares this derivation. But the entire family of this culinary vocabulary, all of which has to do with "cooking," ultimately derives from the Latin verb *coquere*, which means "to cook," and the noun *coquus*, which is Latin for "a cook." The Latin root is *coc*, and interestingly enough, it is also the root of the adjective "precocious." In the 17th century, writers began using this term to describe people who acted especially mature for their ages—as today we use it mostly of children—or pretended to be more sophisticated than they were supposed to be at that particular stage in their lives. Literally, they were "cooked before their time."

How the Oreo Got its Name

Even the good people at the Nabisco Corporation aren't quite sure how the name came about. First invented by the National Biscuit Company (NaBisCo) in 1912—an "Oreo" was a cookie made up of two chocolate disks with a white cream filling. Since its invention in 1912, over 362 billion *Oreo* cookies have been sold, making it the best selling cookie in the history of the United States. But as for its name, get ready for some heavy bullshit.

Some people will tell you that it comes from the French word for gold (*or*) because gold was the dominant color of the package in which the first *Oreos* were sold. Which sounds like pure bullshit, as I'm the sure the process went—1) they made the cookie; 2) then they figured out what to name it; 3) then, based on the name they came up with, they designed the packaging. Not the other way around.

Others claim that the name derives from the Greek word *oreios* (ορειος—say: "oh-rey-ohs") which means "mountain" because it is alleged that an early prototype of the cookie wasn' the flat disc we love so much to dunk in milk today, but was conical in shape—like a mountain. If you want to explore the word's possible classical roots further, you might consider the Greek word *orexis* (ορεξις), which can mean "hunger" in a basic sense but also by extension any kind of appetite, not necessarily just for food.

> **Etymological Note:** If we take the root *orex* and add the "alpha privative" to it—remember we have to insert the letter "n" between the "alpha privative" and the "o" of the root—we come up with the word "anorexia," which literally means "lack of appetite"—albeit a self-induced one.

If you ask enough people, they will tell you things that seem even more utterly ridiculous than what we have already heard above. For example, we might hear that the word *Oreo* comes from taking the letters "re" from the word "cream" and placing them between the two "o's" from the word "chocolate"—quite clever, actually, as if the two "o's" from the word "chocolate" represented the two chocolate discs, and the "re" from "cream" represented the filling between them. Or else, they just "punt" and say that the cookie was named *Oreo* because it was simple, short and easy to pronounce. You decide, since no one else seems to be able to, but have a few while you're at it. Call it "research!"

A Cookie By Any Other Name

Just like the word "apple," a harmless piece of fruit that came to be a derogatory term coined by native Americans to stigmatize their fellow native Americans who "went white" so to speak, so also the word "Oreo"—the name of a cookie that really may have no meaning at all—also came to be a pejorative term coined by African Americans to stigmatize their fellow African Americans whom they perceived as also "going white."

The word "Oreo"—whose name cannot even be explained by the people who created it—suddenly became a badge of shame, a label for someone who is black on the outside but white on the inside. It was first used in this way in a quotation taken from an article in a 1969 edition of *Harpers Bazaar* magazine: "Trouble is Negroes been programmed by white folks to believe their products are inferior. We've developed into a generation of Oreos." In 1970, H. E. Roberts provided a more straightforward definition of "Oreo" as a "black person with white-oriented attitudes." So, there you have it.

What happened to the word "Oreo" is another example of the "artificial" way words change. The scary thing is that the words "apple" and "Oreo" started off meaning one thing and ended up meaning something completely different—and that the shift in meaning had nothing to do with the elements of the word getting "blurred" through usage, over time—in some "natural" way. No, it was a deliberate and malicious change.

What happened to the words "apple" and "Oreo" was altogether different than what happened to the word "hypocrite." But whether we're talking about "apples" or "Oreos," questions like *who* first coined the new derogatory, racist meaning, or *when* they did, or even *why*, are both irrelevant and impossible to answer. For all it mattered, they could have picked a strawberry and an ice cream sandwich to make the same point—what difference would it have made?

There's Nothing like a good Bōk

Let's try an experiment. Take the word "bibliophile" and break it down into its original elements. We find that it is harmless enough, right? It is made up of the Greek root *biblio* from the Greek noun *biblion* (βιβλιον), which means "book," and the suffix "phile" from the Greek verb *phileo* (φιλεω—say: "fi-leh-oh") which means "to like" or "to love." So a "bibliophile" is "someone who likes books." Now—unless you happen to be living in the fictional, futuristic world of Ray Bradbury's

Fahrenheit 451, a novel in which the government has banned all books and anyone caught in possession of one is a considered a criminal—I should think that being labeled a "bibliophile" would be a compliment.

> **Etymological Note:** The expression "to coin"—meaning to make something well known or universally recognized—has nothing to do with "coins," as in the loose change rattling around in your pocket. Most people think that the saying "to coin a phrase..." means to make the phrase "common" or "well-known" by passing it around like loose change gets passed around. Metaphorically, that is. But there's nothing metaphorical about it. The term "coin" derives from the Greek adjective *koinos* (κοινος—say: "koy-noss") which means "common." When the *New Testament* was written, the language they chose was not Aramaic—the Semitic language that was spoken throughout the Near East between around 300 B.C. to around 650 A.D., and the language that Jesus is believed to have spoken. Aramaic was just the language of that particular region, and the writers of the *New Testament* wanted to spread the word beyond that region throughout the Mediterranean world—to the masses. The *New Testament* was written in ancient Greek because Greek was the most widely spoken language of the entire Mediterranean world at that time. In order to popularize this document, they even wrote the *New Testament* in a form of Greek that was especially easy to read—not the classically complex and rhetoricall challenging Greek of Plato or Aristotle—but a simplified version meant for the "common man." The term for this style of Greek was Γραικος *coίνος*, or "common Greek," a form of the language so simple that even the most illiterate fisherman could understand it or at least get the gist of it. This way The Word was sure to spread and become "common."

Now, to get back to our "experiment." Take the word "pediatrician." It comes from two harmless elements we've already discussed: the Greek root *ped* (from παιδος, meaning child) and the suffix "iatrician," which derives from the Greek suffix denoting an adjective for someone or something associated with the medical profession, "iatrikos" (ιατρικος—say: "ee-ah-tri-kos"). So a "pediatrician" is a "children's doctor." Now *there's* a noble profession if there ever was one.

But watch what happens when we take the prefix of the word "*ped*iatrician" and the suffix of "biblio*phile*" and splice them together. We get the word "pedophile." Literally, based on its ingredients, we can only come up with a word that means "someone who likes children." But this is not what the word has come to mean at all.

Question

If he's living up to the ingredients of the word, then a "bibliophile" shouldn't be doing anything strange or sexual with his books, and likewise, a "pediatrician" is only helping children. Well, how then can the word "pedophile," a combination of two elements—one from each of the words mentioned above— mean anything other than "someone who likes" or "is fond of children?"

Answer

In the purest sense, it cannot. If we look the word up in our ancient Greek lexicon, we find that *paidophilia* (παιδοφιλια) means simply what its ingredients mean. Its primary definition—i.e., how it would have been understood by your average ancient Greek—was simply "someone who was fond of children." It is actually an epithet used of Demeter, the goddess of the harvest. There was even an adjectival form *paidophilotera* (παιδοφιλωτερ— say: "peed-oh-fil-oh-tera") that was used of "overprotective" mothers. But at some point it was robbed of its innocence and turned into the monster that it is today. The term "pedophilia" was first used to describe the abnormality of sexual love for a child in 1906 by the psychologist H. Ellis who wrote: "paidophilia, or the love of children…may be included under this head [sc. Abnormality]." The rest is history.

> **Etymological Note:** The Roman name for the Greek goddess Demeter was Ceres. Because Ceres was the goddess of grain and the harvest, it is where we get our word "cereal."

Doing It Greek Style

Now, there is something about ancient Greek culture that makes a lot of people uneasy when they first encounter it, and that is that in classical Greek society, homosexuality was practiced openly. Far from being criticized, it was actually praised. In Plato's *Symposium*, for example, a long dialogue at the end of which Plato concludes that the highest form of love can only exist between a man and another man. And if you study Greek art, you'll see that the relationship was not necessarily betweeen a man and another *man*, but often a boy.

Pedagogy

In ancient Greece, a *paidagogos* (παιδαγωγος—say: "pie-dah-go-gos") was a slave hired by a boy's father to lead his son to school in the morning and bring him home in the afternoon. The word can be broken down into *paidos* (παιδος), the Greek word for child, and the noun *agogos* (αγωγος—say: "ah-go-gos"), the root of which comes from the Greek verb *ago* (αγω—say: "ah-go"), that can mean many different things, depending on the context. In its basic sense, *ago* means simply "to lead." In a military context, for example, it would mean "to lead" an army into battle. Or if you were, say, in a new town and needed a "guide" to show you around, you would hire an *agogos*.

But the verb *ago* can also mean to "to lead away" or "to take for oneself," often in the context of taking a woman in marriage or, by implication, taking away a woman for sexual pleasure. And it's this meaning of *ago* that brings us to the second responsibility placed upon the Greek pedagogue by the father who hired him.

It worked like this: once his son reached the age of puberty—say twelve or so—it was customary for the boy's father to instruct the *paidagogos* to "guide" his son into manhood by sexually educating him in the ways of the ancient Greeks' homosexually fueled society. In other words, to take his kid out back of the woodshed and make him grab his ankles.

This is not to say that men and women didn't marry or screw around. There was marriage, but it was usually strictly for procreative purposes. For sexual satisfaction and true, close companionship, men would generally turn to each other. And it was customary for one of the men to be significantly younger than the other. The custom of there being a disparity in the ages of the male lover and his younger "beloved" is obviously a tradition that arose from the sexual initiation ritual between a young boy and his older pedagogue.

As I mentioned above, we encounter this practice as a common theme in ancient art. Whenever two male lovers are depicted—and it is a *common* motif—the artists always make the disparity in the ages clear, generally by showing one man as bearded and the other not. The decorative motifs of Greek red and black figure pottery from the 5th century B.C. are full of such examples. "The Tomb of the Diver" at Paestum in southern Italy is another exceptional illustration of this social custom. Remember, girls married at the age of twelve, so there is no reason why the sexual marketability of boys didn't begin at this tender age as well.

The amazing thing is that today, the word "pedagogy" is used strictly in the context of education—good, clean classroom teaching. It has lost, entirely, any of the sexual connotations that are right there in the ingredients of the word. Yet "pedophile"—a word that contains nothing immorally sexual about it, that was not understood by the ancient Greeks as having anything to do with child molestation, today has come to mean— and *only* mean—a sexual predator, a monster. And, if found out, the pedophile is soon to be a criminal branded for life. Somewhere along the line, the two words "flip-flopped" in their meaning— or at least in their usage. As a teacher myself, whenever anyone asks me about my "pedagogical" methods, I toy with answering with something along the lines of "Oh, I dunno, handcuffs?" Then I think twice about it and do my best to avoid the question altogether.

Achilles and Partroclus

Most people don't understand that Achilles and Patrolcus, two of the most important characters of Homer's *Iliad*, were raised under the ritual practice of this pedagogical culture, and so shared the homoerotic relationship of "lover" and "beloved" that was so common among men of the period. So when Achilles went to fight at Troy, he brought along with him his "beloved" friend, Patroclus. Generally, it was the "beloved" who was the younger of the two and tended to wear the knee pads in the relationship. But what a lot of people don't know is that it was *Achilles*, not Patroclus, who was the younger, the "beloved"—who "wore the knee pads."

Now, when Achilles refuses to continue to fight for the Greeks over the issue of the girl that Agamemnon took from him, Patroclus, like the rest of his fellow Myrmidons, grows increasingly frustrated at Achilles' obstinacy and becomes increasingly weary of watching his fellow Greeks dying because of Achilles' hubris—for hubris it was for Achilles to take his beef with Agamemnon to such extremes. The Greeks were losing the war because of his unwillingness to "let it go." To be the bigger man. Even when Agamemnon offered to return the girl, Achilles remained obdurate, inflexible, and uncompromising. It was at this point in the poem that Achilles crossed the line and entered the murky land of Hubrisville—not a friendly place, and when you go there, you usually don't go to "visit," you go to *stay*.

Now, each Greek hero had his own custom set of armor, so that he could be identified on the battlefield. Well, one night, Patroclus gets it in his head that if he were to put on Achilles' armor, he could, under the disguise of Achilles, lead the Myrmidons into battle and save the lives of his fellow Greeks. The rest of the Greek army would be so relieved to see that "Achilles" had re-entered the battle, that it just might turn the tide of the war.

So, he does it. Just before dawn, he rises from Achilles' bed, sneaks off and puts on the armor of Achilles thinking that, with his helmet and all, no one would know the difference. And he was right. No one did. Everyone saw the figure of Achilles' armor and thought that it was Achilles inside. Suddenly, the spirit of the Greek army is revived. Patroclus has pulled it off, fooled everyone into thinking *he was* Achilles—including, tragically, himself. Meanwhile, Hector is watching all this from the high walls of Troy, and also thinks that Achilles has returned to the fighting. So he puts on his armor and comes out to fight Achilles—something he's been waiting the past ten years to do!

There's only one small problem. Patroclus might be wearing Achilles armor, he might *look* like Achilles—at this point he may even *think* he's

Achilles—but Achilles he is *not*. And as he and Hector begin to fight, it quickly becomes painfully clear that Patrolcus cannot pull it off. He's no match for Hector, who slays him to the horror of all the Greeks watching as the two mighty warriors pound it out. Then, according to custom, Hector strips the corpse of his armor—the armor of Achilles!—as a war prize. But when Hector removes the helmet, he reveals to the amazement of all those watching, that it was *not* Achilles he had just killed, but Patroclus who was trying to pass himself off as Achilles!

When word reaches Achilles that his Patroclus had been slain by Hector, and that Hector had taken his armor as a prize and was now wearing it himself, Achilles had no choice but to return to the battlefield and fight Hector. Most modern readers of the *Iliad*—and I'm including many teachers here—fail to grasp the enormous emotional impact that the death of Patroclus had on Achilles. Patrolcus was more than simply a "close friend." Achilles and Patroclus weren't just "friends," they were "lovers," in a relationship that was as intimate as that of a man and wife. This is why Patroclus' death adrenalizes Achilles and provides an impetus great enough to cause him to forget all about his beef with Agamemnon and go out to fight Hector in order to avenge the death of Patroclus.

No, I'm still not going to tell you how it turns out. But I will leave you with the image that Homer does. Achilles gets a new suit of armor made for him by Vulcan before he fights Hector. As Achilles is fighting Hector, remember that Hector is wearing Achilles' old armor. Both men, in full armor, would be recognizable to all those watching only by their armor. The Armor of Achilles is so well known to the Greeks that the image of Achilles fighting Hector who is wearing Achilles' old armor, is the picture of Achilles fighting himself. It is a brilliant visual metaphor for Achilles' own internal conflict. Achilles finally realized that it was his own hubris that caused the death of his beloved Patrolcus. Homer leaves us with an incredible image of a man fighting with himself.

Big Hat, Small Herd

Get With The Team!

The coach of our football team used to tell the local papers whenever we lost—and we lost a *lot*—that the offense had been "neither efficient nor effective" in doing its job. Or else it was the defense. Or the special teams. But whatever it was, the phrase that followed remained the same: "neither efficient nor effective." They ended up firing him—not because of saying that (although, they *should* have).

Making Something Happen

If we compare the words "efficient" and "effective," we might be surprised to learn that they mean the same thing because once again they contain the exact same ingredients. If we break down the word "efficient," we get: *ef* + *fic* + *ient*. Now, if we remember what happens when "consonants collide," the prefix "ef" started out as "ex." We dropped the "x" of the prefix and doubled the "f" of the root. We remember now that the root of the word, *fic*, through "vowel shortening," had begun as *fac* from the Latin verb *facere* meaning "to make" or "to do." Adding the prefix "ex" then caused the "a" to shorten to an "i." The suffix "ient" is a common ending that turns a word into an adjective. So what we are left with is *ex • fac • ient*, which means, based on its ingredients, "having the quality of making" (*fac*) something "out of" (*ex*) something else.

If we look at "effective," we should by now be able to recognize the same common elements: *ef* + *fect* + *ive*. Once again, applying our rules about consonants and vowels, "ef" originated as "ex," the root *fect*, before "vowel shortening" occurred, was *fact* (again, from *facere*), and the suffix "ive" like "ient" denotes an adjective. So what we are left with is *ex • fact • ive*, which means, based on its ingredients, "having the quality of making" (*fact*) something "out of" (*ex*) something else.

In terms of football, making the ball land in the arms of a wide receiver charging downfield would be an "efficient" play. An "effective" offense should eventually be able to get that ball in the end zone. And an "effective" defense ought to prevent that from happening. But unfortunately neither our offense nor our defense was "effective." Nor were they "efficient." But to say one of them was *neither* "effective" *nor* "efficient" is to expose your ignorance of the fact that both words mean the same thing. The phrase is a common one you've probably heard and/or used yourself without thinking about it. It's a big, wordy phrase—used by people who wish to sound educated and important. Had our coach concentrated on using big plays instead of big, wordy phrases, he might have kept his job!

Everybody do The Wave!

So, in effect, the words "efficient" and "effective" are redundant. They mean the same thing. Other words built with these ingredients that you should watch out for are "efficacy," a noun, and the adjective "efficacious." They are all made up of *ex* + *fac* + whatever suffix you choose depending on what part of speech you want to make. Like "efficient" and "effective," they are big words that, in terms of football, unfortunately don't translate into big wins.

> **Etymological Note:** The root of the word "redundancy" is *unda*, the Latin word for "wave." The word is a metaphor for the image of how waves continually roll in and out, in and out, endlessly, striking the same stretch of beach over and over and over. Whenever I hear people using redundancies such as these, it puts me in mind of the feeling you get when you find yourself driving behind someone who has left his turn signal on after he's made the turn. You kind of feel sorry for him in a clownish way. It shows that he's not in control of what he's doing.

Irregardless

A classic example of redundancy is the word "irregardless." If we break it down into its elements, we see that it is made up of *ir + regard + less*. Now, remembering our rule about "when consonants collide," the *ir* at the beginning of the word started out as the negatory prefix "in," only when spliced onto *regard*, which begins with a consonant, the "n" drops off of "in" to be replaced by the "r" of the root. The problem is that the word also has the suffix, "less," which also negates. So "irregardless" contains both a prefix and a suffix that negate its root. The correct word is "regardless," but you'll hear people using "irregardless" all the time because it is a bigger word, and when people use big words, they feel it makes them sound more important and intelligent.

What's your Shoe Size?

There is a term for doing this—for using big words. It's called "sesquipedalianism." Now *there's* a word for you. It comes from the Latin prefix *sesqui* which means "one and a half" and the root *ped* from the Latin adjective *pedalis* meaning "of or pertaining to the foot," plus the suffix "ism" which forms nouns that mean "the act or practice of." So, "sesquipedalianism" means the practice of using (words) that are a foot and a half long. And if we change the suffix "ism" to "ist," we form a noun that means "one who..." So watch out for "sesquipedalianists," because they're usually using big words to cover up for the fact that they really don't know what they're talking about, or they're trying to intimidate or impress you for some reason. Once again, a good rule to remember: never use "utilize" when you can use "use"—and you can *always* use "use."

There's a Time to Pare Down, and a Time to Pair Up

Knowing *when* is the trick. Very few words—such as irregardless—are redundant in and of themselves. Most often redundancies by their very nature are phrases—that is, a pair of words that mean the same thing yet get coupled together—like "efficient and effective." Another favorite of mine, and of former Secretary of State Madeline Albright during the U.N. inspection crisis in Iraq, is the phrase "free and unfettered." You don't need to have had the experience of being handcuffed to know that "free" means "unfettered!" Want another? How about "eligible bachelor?" As we learned in Chapter Six, the word "bachelor" has its roots in the academic term "baccalaureate." Although it wasn't until recently that the word "bachelor" came to mean an unmarried man. Today that's what it means, and that's *all* it means. So by definition, every "bachelor" is "eligible."

> **Minor Etymological Note:** Our word "phrase" comes from the Greek verb *phrazo* (φραζω—say: "fra-dso") which means "to speak" or "to say."

Home Economics

Often referred to as "Home Ec." on high school and college campuses (back in the days when it was still taught), you don't get more redundant than this. The word "economics" comes from the Greek words *oikos* (οικος—say: "oi-koss") which means "home" or "house" + *nomos* (νομος—say: "noh-moss") which means "law." So our term "economics" literally means the "laws of the house." The way it got its meaning of having to do with the management of a business is because in the ancient world, every household *was* a business. If you lived out in the country, then you more than likely maintained a family farm and what you produced fed your family, and what your family didn't consume, you hauled into town and sold in the Agora, the famous marketplace of ancient Athens.

If you lived in a town or a city like Pompeii, for example, your house tended to have at least two or three shops fronting the street, so every homeowner also ran one or several businesses out of his house.

Rules And Regulations

Our word "rule" comes from the Latin noun *regula*, which means "a rule." As the word evolved through French and Old English, it lost the "g" and became *reule*, eventually to become our word "rule." But we have so many rules that one word wasn't enough to cover them all, so we went ahead and put the "g" back in to make a new word—"regulation." But by using the phrase "rules and regulations," you're not only using two words that mean the same thing, they *are* the same thing! Just do yourself a favor. You'll hear people using this phrase—and others like it—often. When you do—as hard as it will be—resist the temptation to correct them. People, as a "rule," don't like to have their grammar corrected. Since "wordiness," then, can be considered another form of "sesquipedalianism," here's another rule for you: never use two words when one will do—especially if they mean the *same thing*!

Report Back

The word "report" is made up of the prefix "re" which means "back" and the root *port* from the Latin verb *portare* which means "to carry." So "report" all on its own means "to carry back." Just like the word "irregardless," the first part of the first word ("re")—which already means "back"—does the trick all by itself. Simply say: "Report to me," and you'll be fine.

Tyrannosaurus Rex

The Tyrannosaurus Rex was considered the scariest of all the dinosaurs. Now, the word "dinosaur" comes from the Greek adjective *deinos* (δεινος—say: "die-noss") which means "scary," and *sauros* (σαυρος—say: "sau-ross") which means "lizard." So, the dinosaurs were just "scary lizards." *Big* scary lizards, too. And the Tyrannosaurus Rex was the scariest lizard of them all.

> **Etymological Note:** The primary meaning of the Greek adjective *deinos* is actually "clever" but with the implication of "cunning" as well. To the ancient Greek mind, "clever" or "cunning" people could get the better of you and so they were also considered "scary." Because of that, you tried to avoid such individuals. Men found this quality in women especially "scary." *Deinos* is the adjective that Euripides often uses of Medea, who was a foreign woman and considered to have "witchy" powers that the Greeks naturally feared. And rightly so, for she caused a bloodbath at the end of Euripides' play that makes Lizzy Borden look like a Girl Scout!

While Paleontologists debate whether or not the Tyrannosaurus Rex stood upright, could run very fast, was a vegetarian, or even had feathers, they named it the "king" of the dinosaurs. The problem is that they named him "king" twice. "Tyrannos" (τυραννος—say: "too-rah-noss")—where we get our word "tyrant"—is the Greek word for "absolute ruler" or "king." Likewise, the word *rex* is the Latin word for "king." And just as τυραννος had a negative connotation among the ancient Greeks, so did the word *rex* as far as the Romans were concerned, because like the Greeks, they had a democratic government in which the people elected their officials.

Party Time!

It's a scary prospect for those who take their politics seriously, but the words "democracy" and "republic" are—sorry to have to break it to you—also redundant. The word "democracy" comes from the Greek word *demos* (δημος—say: "day-moss") which is a collective noun and means "the people," and *kratos* (κρατος—say: "crah-toss") which means "power." So "democracy" means "power by the people" because the people had the power of the vote. The word "republic" is actually a Latin translation of the Greek word "democracy." The word "republic" comes from the Latin noun *res*, which means "thing," and *publicus*, an adjective where we obviously get the word "public"—but it is actually a derivation of the Latin word *populus*, which means "people." So, literally, the word "republic" means "the people's thing."

Ironically, today these two words *could not* be considered more opposite in nature.

Pumping up

Today, with the rising price of gasoline showing no signs of going the other way anytime soon, more and more people are driving off after pumping their gas without paying. To protect themselves against such thievery, the operators of many gas stations post signs now that read: "Please Prepay Before You Pump." The redundancy here is more malodorous than the gasoline to which it refers because the prefix "pre" already means "before." So if you happen to manage a gas station, simply put up a sign that reads: "Please Pay Before You Pump." It may not protect you from "drive-offs," but you'll be doing a big part in helping to put an end to cultural illiteracy!

When a customer *does* pay for his gas and uses a debit card to do so, the attendant will no doubt ask for him to enter his "PIN number." In this case, the word PIN is an acronym. The word acronym comes from the Greek word *akro* (ακρο—say: "ah-crow") which means "high" or "top," and the Greek word *onyma* (ονυμα—say: "on-oo-mah") which means "name." So literally, an "acronym" is a word made up of the "first" letters of a phrase to reduce to a single word an entire concept. The only rule when forming an acronym is that it has to be a word you can pronounce. Like SCUBA—for "Self Contained Underwater Breathing Apparatus"—or NASCAR—for "National Association of Stock Car Auto Racing," etc. PIN is an acronym for "Personal Identification Number." So to ask for one's "PIN number" is about redundant as you can get.

Athletic Scholarship

There's something about this phrase that smacks of redundancy. Let's start with the adjective "athletic," meaning "of or pertaining to an athlete." The problem then becomes how to define the word "athlete." Whenever I ask my class if Tiger Woods, for example, is an "athlete," half the class says "yes," and the other half says "no." Obviously they're not sure if golf, being as slow-paced and non-combative a game as it is, qualifies those who play it as being "athletes." So just what *does* qualify? Is it the type of equipment the individual uses? Whether the sport he plays involves a ball? If she is part of a team, or wears any kind of uniform? Sweating? Running? Jumping? These are usually the kinds of issues that run through someone's mind when pondering this question. Few would agree, for example, that the winner of last year's International Chess Tournament would qualify for an "athletic scholarship"—even if he moved his pieces around the board while wearing cleats, shoulder pads, and a helmet.

But he should. Why? Chess or golf, baseball or bowling—all who participate in these activities *are* "athletes." And here's why: the word "athlete" is nearly a direct transliteration of the Greek noun *athletes* (αθλητης—say: "ath-lay-tase"). The word αθλητης—bear with me on the Greek here—is made up of two elements: 1) the Greek noun *athlon* (αθλον), which means prize; and 2) the suffix "ητης" which means "one who" does or participates in whatever the root of the word means. It comes into English as the suffix "ete" and, though not as common as some of the other "occupational suffixes" (i.e., "or," or "er," or "ist,"), retains its original connotation of "one who…" So an αθλητης—our word "athlete"—is anyone "who competes for a prize." A "competitor." It can be the World Cup or a gold medal or green sport jacket—or just a letter from your university saying you received a scholarship. Most scholarships—if not all, at least on some level—are things you have to apply for, so there's always a chance you might get turned down. There's never enough money for everyone. So a "scholarship" is, by its very nature, "competitive." Like an "athlete" by his very nature. It's the same sort of redundancy as found in the phrases "future prospects," or "past history." Is there *another* kind of history?

Historical Note: Many people believe that it was the Greeks who invented the concept of "competition." But it's not that simple a question. The root of the word "competition" is *pet*, from the verb *petere*, which means "to seek" as in the word "petition." The prefix "com" derives from the Latin preposition *cum* which means "with" or "together." It would be hard not to see that it is part of the human condition to compete, and that it may very well have been the key to the survival of our species. There is some credence to the idea that it was the Greeks who first tapped into this most basic instinct and gave it a formal setting—namely, the Olympic Games—to which they added rules and used them as a form of both entertainment and diplomacy.

Nine Words (And A Fish) You Thought You Knew

Loose Ends

In this chapter I will try to clear up some of the confusion, misconceptions, and general ignorance shared by many people about some of the more common "Words of the Day." Most,
—if not all—will be familiar to you. You will find that you have been using many of them without any real idea either of what the word means or how it got that way. But not to worry—probably no one has noticed because chances are most everybody else has been doing the same thing!

Latin 101

First, here's a little technical stuff. Latin is an "inflected" language. That is, nouns have different endings called "cases" to indicate how they will function in a sentence. For example, the "nominative" case is always the subject; the "accusative" case is usually the direct object; the "dative" case the indirect object, etc. English still retains some remnants of this system—though very few. "Who," for example, is "nominative" whereas "whom" is "accusative." There is also a case called the "genitive," which shows possession. In English we would say "whose" for the "genitive" of the pronoun "who." The "genitive" case is also important because in Latin it contains the "root" of the word, whereas the "nominative" usually does not.

For example, if you looked up the word for "law" in a Latin dictionary, you would be given the "nominative" and the "genitive" cases. It would look like this: "*lex, legis,* law." The way you get to the root of a noun in Latin is to go the genitive form and drop off the last vowel and anything after it. The root then would be *leg*, taken from the genitive. So all derivatives are built on the root: "legal," "legality," "legislature," etc. The same is true for all other words in Latin. The

179

Latin word for night is *nox*. If you looked up *nox* in a Latin dictionary, you would find the entry: "*nox, noctis*, night." The root is *noct*, where we get words like "nocturne," and "nocturnal."

It works the exact same way in Greek. As we discussed earlier, the Latin word *nox* is actually a rip off from the Greek word νυξ, whose genitive is νυκτος from which we get the root νυκτ, which, after transliteration, becomes *nyct*. So it is from "nyct" that we get terms like "nyctophobia," which means "fear" (*phob*) "of the night, or dark" (*nyct*).

Whew!

Glad that's over. Wasn't so bad, was it? You might want to actually learn Latin or ancient Greek one day. Either way, just remember: when you look up a noun in a Latin or Greek dictionary, you are always given the "nominative" and the "genitive" cases because it is the "genitive" case that contains the "root" of the word. How did we get this far into the book without having to tackle this? Because usually the nominative and the genitive are so similar that I was able to spare you the gory details. But we're about to discuss Jupiter again, and the nominative and the genitive of Jupiter do not look anything alike. Always leave it up to old Jupiter to cause trouble! For example, in Latin, "Jupiter" is spelled with two "p's": *Juppiter*. We spell it with one "p" (Jupiter). Don't ask me why.

1) Jovial

Most people know that "jovial" means "happy," or "joyful," but they don't know why. The "genitive" form of the Latin noun *Juppiter* is *Jovis*, so boil it down and we get "jov" as the root of the name of the King of the Gods.

So why is Jupiter always "jovial?" Not just because it is the root of the genitive of his name, but because, as we have already discussed, he had this obsession with ravaging young Earth girls (and, as we'll see, boys), which I suppose beat hanging around Mt. Olympus all day watching *The Wide World of Αθλητης."*

Ganymede: The largest of the Jovian moons, larger even than the planet Mercury, was named Ganymede after a young boy of extreme beauty with whom Jupiter fell madly in love. Taking the form of an Eagle, he swooped down to Earth, snatched him up, and carried him off to Olympus where he made him his personal "cupbearer." Now I don't know what, exactly, a "cupbearer" did up there on Mt. Olympus, but I'm sure at some point it involved knee pads!

- **Io:** The second largest of the Jovian moons was named after Io. As one version of the story goes, Jupiter saw Io walking near a river and fell madly in love with her. He told her to meet him in the woods at noon. When they hooked up, he spread a huge dark cloud over them so that his wife, Juno, wouldn't be able to see what he was up to. But Juno, by now used to her husband's feeble attempts at concealing his extracurricular "amusements," came down to disperse the cloud and expose the lovers. Acting just in time, Jupiter turned Io into a heifer, hoping to fool his wife.

Now, Juno was no fool, but she could play dumb with the best of them, so she complimented her husband on the beautiful heifer he must have found "for her" and asked if she can have it as a gift. What could Jupiter do but give it up? She then sent Argus, a character with a hundred eyes, to keep a constant watch over the heifer in case Jupiter tried to sneak back and free Io from her bondage as a cow. Io remained a heifer for many years but eventually escaped the watchful eyes of Argus and wandered all the way to Egypt. Jupiter felt so bad about all of this that he pleaded with his wife to turn her back into a woman again, which she did on the condition that Jupiter keep his hands off. From then on, Io was worshipped as the Egyptian goddess Isis.

- **Europa:** The third largest of the Jovian moons was named after Europa. Jupiter saw Europa playing with her friends in a meadow by the sea and fell madly in love with her. This time, he took on the form of a big, white, muscular bull and started to prance around in the meadow over near where the little girls were playing in order to attract their attention. Which, of course, he did. Over they came, and he lay down and let them stroke his belly. Then, one by one, he started to give them rides around the meadow. When Europa's turn came and on she climbed, he bolted straight for the sea where he transported her to the island of Crete. There, under the shade of a Plane tree, they made crazy love. She must have been some piece of ass, because old Jupiter had such a good time that he named an entire continent after her.

- **Callisto:** The fourth of the Jovian moons was named after Callisto (whose name in ancient Greek really does transliterate to τη καλλιςτη—but don't tell Aphrodite!). Callisto was a follower of Demeter, the virgin goddess, and vowed to remain a virgin for a life of service to the goddess. But Jupiter fell madly in love with her and put an end to all of that nonsense. Having learned from the Io episode, after he was done with Callisto he turned her into a bear so that Juno wouldn't find out (why a bear would be any better than a cow is anybody's guess), but you can't fool your wife even if your name is Zeus, so Juno convinced Demeter to shoot the "bear," on the grounds that Callisto had to be punished for breaking her vow of celibacy. Jupiter felt so bad about all this that he turned Callisto into the constellation Ursa Major. Juno was so pissed off that Callisto had been given this honor that she persuaded Ocean (who was a god as well a river that the ancients believed encircled the earth which, of course, was at that time flat) never to let her touch his waters, so that Callisto would have no rest. She was a constellation doomed to circle the pole star without ever setting.

2) Idiot

In ancient Greece, if you wanted to vote, you had to appear in person in a large city center like, say, Athens, and vote there. There were no polling stations or absentee ballots. So if you were a farmer living out on your spread some five or ten miles from town and you wanted to vote, you first of all had to drop everything you were doing on the farm—and there was always plenty to do down on the farm—and make what was probably a two to three day round trip journey while you left you wife and children at home alone to fend for themselves.

Travel in the ancient world could be a brutal experience. Remember, this was long before there was anything like a police force or a highway patrol, so there were plenty of people out there just waiting for you to come riding down the road so they could beat you over the head and rob you blind—and that was if you were *lucky*! And what if you had to spend the night along the way? Motels back then just weren't what they are today—which *still* isn't saying much! The technology of the lock and key had been invented, but far from perfected, so there was a good chance that if you spent the night at an "inn," you'd wake up to find not only your shoes and clothes and money stolen, but also your horse, or donkey, or mule and whatever was hitched onto the back of it. A good mule and wagon—let alone a horse—could bring a lot of drachma on the black market. Plus, people didn't ask too many questions when the price was right.

As a result, many farmers living out in the boonies just figured the heck with it and didn't bother to risk getting robbed or worse just to drop a pottery shard into an urn with someone's name on it. Besides, what did he care who was the ruling Archon in Athens any given year? Did it really affect him? As a result, a lot of these people just kept to themselves and didn't get involved in politics simply because it was so impractical—not to mention dangerous—for them to try.

In ancient Greece, a person who kept to himself and out of public life was referred to as an *idiotes* (ιδιοτης—say: "id-ee-oh-tase"). The noun derives from the adjective *idios* (ιδιος—say: "id-ee-ohs"), meaning "private," and the "occupational suffix" "της" meaning "person who does something" (remember αθλητης?). Over time, it began to take on a pejorative meaning because people who did not get involved with public life were seen as "ignorant" or even "simple-minded." Imagine a person who never picks up a newspaper or watches a single news broadcast, and you can see how the word began to change. To say "He's an idiot," was to say that that person didn't know what was going on. By the mid 14th century, it could mean anything from simply an "uneducated person" to a "feeble-minded fool."

Plato Was an Idiot?

You might find it interesting that before it began to take on the pejorative social baggage that it has today, the ancient Greeks often used the word ιδιοτης of a writer who wrote prose as opposed to poetry. This was because poetry was written to be read aloud and performed in public, but prose, such as the philosophical writings of Plato, were generally intended to be read silently and contemplated in private.

> **Historical Note:** The way you voted in ancient Greece worked like this: you were handed a small piece of broken pottery— called a shard—on which you wrote, or scratched, the name of your candidate, and then dropped the shard into an urn. The Greek word for this kind of a pottery shard was *ostrakon* (οστρακον—say: "oh-strah-con"). And because this was the same process that the Greeks used to remove someone from office—or even from society if they felt the person had committed a crime and needed to be exiled—our term "to *ostracize*" derives from this ancient custom.

3) Money

Way back in the 6th and 5th centuries B.C., Rome was still little more than just a wide space in the "salt road"—the pathway that the people living in the mountains followed to get to the salt pans at the mouth of the Tiber—and its economy was based on the tolls these early Romans charged at their bridges so people journeying from the hills to the sea could cross the river. Sometime around in there, the Romans also started setting up little shops and stalls along the road leading up to the bridge, in case someone wanted to buy a spare rib or a hot dog or grab a little vino along the way. These migrating people paid in *sal,* the Latin word for salt, hence the term *salary.*

Eventually, the Romans established an economy that, like the Greeks before them, was based on three basic metals: bronze; silver; and gold. They developed their own "coinage" and assigned value based on the weight of the metal in the coin. Obviously bronze coins were worth less than silver coins, which were worth less than gold, and so on. To strike coins, you needed a secure place to store and weigh the metals, strike them into individual coins, etc., and so the Romans set up a mint in the Temple of Juno on the Capitoline Hill, which had the steepest slopes of the original Seven Hills of Rome and thus was the most easily defended.

Sometime around the turn of the third century B.C., just as the Romans were getting their shit together, they were suddenly invaded by the Gauls. The Romans took up a defensive position on the Capitoline hill, and the Gauls surrounded it. The siege lasted for a few days until one night the Gauls tried to scale the steep slope of the hill in order to catch the Romans off-guard. Unfortunately for them, they chose the side of the hill where the Temple of Juno stood. What the Gauls didn't know was that all around the temple, the flock of the Sacred Geese of Juno were sleeping, as were most of the Romans. As the first of the Gauls reached the top of the hill, they awoke the Sacred Geese who started quacking up a storm. The quacking of the Sacred Geese in turn awoke the Romans, who were then easily able to fend off the Gauls from the top of the hill.

As it turned out, the Gauls weren't all that interested in occupying Rome. They were just curious about these strange people who wore togas and had long beards, so they had come down to have a look. So after a little slaughtering, raping, and pillaging, they said the heck with it and went back home and forgot all about Rome. But Rome would not forget about them…

Because the Sacred Geese around Juno's temple had warned the sleeping Romans of the stealthy approach of the Gauls, they renamed it the Temple of Juno Moneta, her new nickname taken from the verb *monere*, which means "to warn." So from then on, her temple was known as the Temple of Juno the "Warner." Because it was also in the Temple of Juno Moneta that the Romans continued to coin their money, the coins that were struck there were referred to as *moneta* in Latin. This "nickname" is obviously also where we get words like "monetary."

Historical Note: The images societies put on their money can often have far-reaching affects. The early Romans, as the Greeks before them, didn't shave and were known for their beards. Until Alexander the Great, that is. Alexander had a quarrelsome relationship with his father, Philip II of Macedon, who also wore a beard. Alex and daddy didn't get along because Philip, a notorious drunk and womanizer, slept with everyone but the family mule—not that he probably hadn't *tried*—and this upset Alex's mother Olympias. Alex and his mother were very close. In order to get back at Philip, Olympias took to sleeping with snakes in her bed, hoping that Philip might happen to remember where it was and show up one night. He never did. But because Philip was a mean guy and an even meaner drunk—which he was most of the time—there wasn't much Alex could do in the rebelliousness of his youth but to shave. And then go on to conquer the world! Right before Alex left to do just that, Philip was murdered. Most scholars agree that Alexander had absolutely *nothing* to do with it whatsoever.

As Alexander conquered the world, he had to pay his army, so he struck a lot of coins that bore his face on one side and an image of Zeus on the other. These coins circulated quickly throughout the Mediterranean world and eventually fell into the hands of the Romans, who were so impressed with Alexander's military conquests that they all wanted to be just like him. Thus, the trend of shaving became all the rage. Whether or not Alexander "conquered the world," one thing is certain: he set a new vogue for the men of ancient Rome that would endure for centuries!

4) Orgy

Our word "orgy" derives directly from the Greek noun *orge* (οϱγη—say" "or-gay"), which was their word for "anger." But the ancient Greeks didn't differentiate between emotions quite the same way we do. They saw any emotion that caused you to lose control of yourself, that caused you to do something completely beyond the realm of your normal behavior, as a manifestation of οϱγη. When, for example, you read in the paper about the latest "road rage" incident in which someone otherwise calm and reasonable suddenly turns into a murderous maniac after being cut off by another driver—*that* would be a good example of how the Greeks understood the word *orge*. Our word "anger" severely limits the scope of *orge*. To the ancient Greeks, it could be any emotion—"anger," "passion," "lust"—that caused you to lose your ability to think clearly.

Many of the Greek gods and goddesses were on one level simply walking metaphors for these strong, passionate emotions. Zeus obviously represented "power," whose seductive sway the Greeks were very aware—and wary—of. It was, for example, the aspiration of being king that seduced Oedipus and brought him to his ruinous end. Aphrodite embodied the carnal, sexual passions. Artemis, just the opposite—she was a virginal goddess, who represented the power of abstinence and self-control which, when taken to extremes, could turn to "sanctimony," another no-no. Read Euripdes' play *Hippolytus* if you want to see what happens to someone whose disdain for sex causes his downfall. Each one of the gods and goddesses represented a potential *orge* which, if taken too far, could destroy you. The idea was to "worship" each god and goddess equally, not to extremes and not to the exclusion of one or another, but treat them all equally. In other words, lead a balanced life.

It's hardly news that the ancient Greeks were very fond of wine and were very proud of their vintages. But they were also aware of how powerful and dangerous the effects of drinking too much of it could be. The god Bacchus (also known as Dionysus) was the god they invented for this particular *orge*. His followers were called the Bacchae—a troop of women who followed him around in the woods along with these creatures called Satyrs who were half man and half goat and whose leader was named Silenus. It was a secret cult. You could be initiated into it only after "spiritual purification" by being allowed to take part in one of their "orgiastic" rituals that involved, first and foremost, the consumption of wine until you had lost control of your senses. After that, anything could happen. Usually, it was sexual in nature, but things could also get a little rough. There is a "rough" side to raw, sexual, aggression. A very "physical" aggression.

Today, our word "orgy" simply retains the "group sex" idea for most people, but for the Greeks, the sexual aspect of the cult was only incidental, secondary. It was the loss of control that was "orgiastic" about these sorts of activities. The root *org* is also where we get our word "orgasm," which is, literally, a loss of control, is it not? Sometimes it happens when—*ooops!*—you *least* expect or even want it to. Sometimes, it just doesn't "come" at all.

> **Etymological Note:** Our expression "to come." meaning to experience orgasm, derives from the Latin verb *venire*, which means "to come"—primarily in the sense of "to arrive"—but still, the root of the word is *ven*, and it is from *this* root that the Roman goddess *Venus* derives her name. Venus was the Roman counterpart of the Greek goddess Aphrodite, and like Aphrodite, was a metaphor for the power of raw sexuality. *Ven*ereal diseases are sexually transmitted, contracted through the "sexchange" of bodily fluids when you "come."

5) Pornography

It was a sad day for all who strive for precision with words when, in 1964, Supreme Court Justice Potter Stewart tried to explain the word "pornography" when concurring in Jacobellis v. Ohio by saying he could *not* define it: "I shall not today attempt further to define the kinds of material I understand to be embraced within that shorthand description; and perhaps I could never succeed in intelligibly doing so. But I know it when I see it." Justice Stewart obviously should have consulted his Greek lexicon, where he would have found that the word "pornography," derives from the Greek root *porn* (from the noun πορνη—say "por-nay"), which was their term for "prostitute" or "whore" and *graph,* which comes from the Greek verb γραφω (say: "grah-foe"), and can mean anything along the lines of "to write," or, "to paint," or "to draw."

> **Etymological Note:** Some of the most beautiful artifacts to survive from ancient Greece are the black and red figure terra-cotta vases, pots, and cups I have mentioned before. Generally, the artist who painted the pot was a different individual than the man who made the pot. Often one or the other—or both upon occasion—would sign the pot. The painter would use this verb —γραφω—when he signed the pot. The man who made the pot, who "threw" the clay upon a wheel turned by a crank-like device either operated by the foot of the maker himself, or by an apprentice, used the verb *poieo* (ποιεω—say: "poi-eh-owe"), which means, literally, "to make." The noun ποιητης (say: "poi-yey-tase") that derives from this verb is where we get the word *"poet,"* which means, literally, anyone who makes or creates something. By the time the Romans got a hold of it and transliterated it into the Latin noun *poeta,* it was used primarily as we use it today: of one who creates verse, or "poetry."

So the definition of "pornography" is the "depiction of a prostitute." Period. The small seaside town of Pompeii, for example, began as an early Greek settlement and became a resort town for wealthy Romans by the 1st century B.C. Pompeii was destroyed in the year 79 A.D., following the eruption of Mt. Vesuvius, and is still being excavated today—in fact, it is the oldest ongoing archaeological site in the world. In its heyday, at the time of its destruction, it had a population of about 20,000 people, give or take. And even though there are still large parts of the city that have yet to be excavated, to date they have found evidence of 174 houses of prostitution. That's a pretty large number for such a small town, and there are doubtless others yet to be discovered.

The Latin term for "prostitute" is *lupa* (which, interestingly, also means "she-wolf"), and the word for a "whorehouse" is *lupanar*. When you entered a *lupanar*, you were presented with a "menu," as it were. This menu was usually painted on the walls, often near the entrance, and showed the various sexual "specialties of the house" that were available, and what each one cost. These pictures were, literally, *pornographia*, because they showed what sorts of prostitutes plied their trade there, as each usually had his or her own "specialty." One *lupa* might specialize in fellatio, another might take it up the ass. The price varied from one type of "servicing" to another and from one *lupanar* to the next, depending upon the neighborhood, quality of the work, etc.

> **Historical Note:** Unlike our modern society, where prostitution is looked down upon and—with a few exceptions—criminalized, this was not the case in the ancient world. Unlike today, it also was not a service offered primarily by women for men. A woman could also be "serviced" at a *lupanar*. And in fact, many often were. Most *lupanaria* featured a "cunnilinguist" for their female clientele. There was apparently one man who was extremely skilled at it, and he seemed to work on a "free lance" type basis as archaeologists have found his name featured in advertisements painted on the walls of several of these establishments. It would seem from the evidence that the Romans considered "cunt lapping" an art that took great skill to master and perform correctly—and you know…they were *right*!

6) Fornication

If the ancient Greeks were known for anything—and what *weren't* they known for?—it was for their skill as master architects. They knew how to move stone. Like the ancient Egyptians—who many feel taught them—they were famous for their ability to design great monuments out of stone—often quarried and hauled overland for hundreds of miles. These monuments were carved and erected using a technology that today we would consider little more sophisticated than toothpicks and bobby pins. And yet, many of them are still standing—albeit in one state of ruin or another—as a testament to the enduring effort of man. Why they chose to spend their lives toiling in this way, instead of, say, just going to the beach—and Greece has some beautiful beaches!—we will never know. Like the pyramids of ancient Egypt, the temples of ancient Greece stand like silent sentinels to the legacy of the persistence and endurance of human industry.

But for all that they achieved with chisel and mallet, the Greeks were forever locked into what is known as "post and lintel" architecture. That is, erect a column, erect a second one next to it, and connect them by lowering a rectangular block of stone across the space between them. Simply repeat this process over and over, and you have the beginnings of your standard Greek temple. Just think of it as framing a house only using marble instead of maple.

The "post and lintel" technique was fine for your traditional Greek style temple—such as the Parthenon, which still crowns the summit of the Acropolis in Athens and represents perhaps the pinnacle of Greek architectural genius. It is, along with the Eiffel Tower, the Statue of Liberty, the Colosseum and the Sphinx that guards the pyramids on the Giza plateau along the bank of the Nile, arguably one of the most universally recognizable man-made structures in the world.

At first, the Romans copied the Greek style of "post and lintel" architecture. Many of the early temples in the Roman forum, such as the Temple of Saturn and the Temple of Castor—two of the oldest temples in Rome dating back to the turn of the 5th century B.C.—were built using the post and lintel design. The only problem with the post and lintel style is that no matter how close you align your columns—no matter now narrow the intercolumniation, no matter how thick and sturdy the lintel that spans it—you can only put so much stress on that lintel before it will crack.

This inherent design flaw prevented both the Greeks and the early Romans from building much higher than a first—or in some limited cases a small, lightweight second story—not much more than a terrace really—simply because the post and lintel design could not bear the weight of any substantial superstructure. It was the Romans who developed the solution to this problem, around 100 B.C.: the arch. They had actually been already using the arch for over a century, but for a different purpose.

Aqueducts and Arches

For most of its life, a Roman aqueduct is simply a pipe buried underground that carries water from the Apennine Mountains to Rome and other urban centers. It is only when the pipe gets close to its destination that it begins to rise out of the ground. The reason for this is simple physics. By the time a great volume of water has traveled some three or four hundred kilometers downhill, it has built up a great amount of velocity that must be dissipated somehow, otherwise the water pressure will be uncontrollable and impossible to harness. The easiest way to alleviate the pressure was by using the natural force of gravity—by reversing the slope that carried the water downhill and created all the pressure in the first place.

This is where the arch becomes instrumental. By using the arch to raise the pipe out of the ground and then bumping up the height of each arch by small increments, the Romans could carry the water into the city on a row of arches marching in advancing height to slow down the flow of the water. In this way, Roman engineers created and maintained a water pressure that was controllable, so that by the time it reached its destination, it could be put to practical use.

Amphitheatres and Arches

Constructing an arch to carry the weight of a pipe full of water was one thing. Its purpose was to elevate and cover distance—not necessarily to support a lot of weight. Were it not for the arch, engineering feats such as the Circus Maximus and the Colosseum, not to mention practically every other theatre the Romans built, would have been impossible. The Roman were running water over arches for over a hundred years before it dawned on them that the arch was capable of much, much more.

Terracina

It would not be until the turn of the first century before Christ that— at a remote site some fifty kilometers south of Rome on the Via Appia, in a town by the sea called Terracina—that Roman engineers realized the true versatility of the arch and its importance as a structural device. The way the arch works—the reason it can support such loads—is that the *voussoirs* (wedge shaped blocks at the curve of the shoulders of the arch) were held in place by the keystone—also wedge-shaped—so that the thrust of any weight placed on top of it would be transferred

194

equally through the shoulders of the arch and down each side to be absorbed by the foundation.

While Romans were exploring the possibilities of the arch, they stumbled upon something else—that if they mixed a little sand, gravel, water, and some Pozzuoli volcanic ash together, a chemical reaction would occur that would cause it to harden into something we call today "concrete." And with a little more time and refinement of the process, they eventually could get their concrete to set underwater! By constructing wooden frames in the shape of arches and pouring concrete over top of them, they could manufacture a substructure of arches that could carry a superstructure as high as their imaginations allowed them to—and do it very quickly as well.

It was the design of the arch, along with the invention of concrete, that enabled the Romans to build on a scale not even dreamed of by the Greeks. Ironically, at Terracina, the Romans used the marriage of these two newfound technologies in order to construct a level platform on the uneven surface of the top of a mountain in order to build a traditional post and lintel style temple.

Caesar, the Architect

It wouldn't be until about fifty years later that none other than Julius Caesar recognized the arch for something more than simply an architectural apparatus that enabled the Romans to build sturdy foundations. Aside from being a brilliant military commander, Caesar was a man of true vision and saw the aesthetic beauty in the simplicity of its shape, and designed a building on a grand scale that—instead of hiding the arches under the building as a support system—featured them by stacking three tiers of open arches, one on top of the other. Once completed, the building would end up accommodating 150,000 people. That building was the Circus Maximus—rightly named as the "greatest arena" for chariot racing in the entire ancient world. Charioteers would travel from as far away as Egypt and Syria, just to brag that they had raced in the "greatest circus in the world!"

Chariot racing in the valley between the Palatine and Aventine hills in Rome dates back at least to the 7th century B.C. Probably spectators sat on the surrounding hills, or erected make-shift wooden bleachers to watch the teams of four-horse chariots—called *quadrigae*—race around the valley.

But it was Julius Caesar who transformed the place from a field surrounded by wooden bleachers on the hillsides encircling the valley, to a monumental stone structure that was 700 meters long, three tiers high, and could seat up to 150,000 spectators. And he could not have done it without the technology of the arch and concrete.

Going "Arching"

The Romans loved Caesar for building the Circus Maximus, especially since he funded the whole project personally from the "killing" he was making as provincial governor of Gaul from 59 to 50 B.C.

Watching a chariot race was about as much fun as you could have in a city like Rome—twelve teams of four horse chariots charging through the dust, lap after lap, crashing into each other, bodies flying everywhere. But chariot racing didn't go on every day. Rather, they only occurred during festivals. And the Circus Maximus, due to the nature of its construction—with all those open, exposed archways— invited people to move in and set up shops in the archways, often with the shopkeeper living above his shop. It wasn't long before the place became a virtual outdoor mall. One of the most popular commodities sold in these archways was sex, and some scholars estimate that one out of every three to five archway shops was a house of prostitution, or was home to some other lewd activity to be had for a price. This was probably the reason why so many of Rome's fires began in the vicinity of the Circus Maximus—some old whore knocking over a lamp and setting her straw mattress on fire.

So if you were in the market for that kind of thing, the arches of the Circus Maximus were where you went. The Latin word for arch is *fornix*, and the root is *fornic*. So if you are going to go "fornicate" literally, you are going to go "arching," and if that was the case, chances were you were looking for *one* thing and if it was "head," you can bet your ass it wasn't head of "lettuce!"

7) Sinister

The word "sinister" comes into English directly from the Latin adjective *sinister* which means "left-handed" or of anything "occurring on the left." This is opposed to the adjective *dexter*, which means "right handed" or anything "occurring on the right." Now the idea of left-handed people being considered unlucky or ill-omened is no longer a modern concept, but it *was* in antiquity, and that particular connotation dates back to the earliest of the ancient Roman days. Because most people were—as they are today—right-handed, the Romans viewed left-handed people as oddballs, abnormal, and unlucky. The reason they cared so much about this kind of stuff was that the ancient Romans—like the Greeks before them—were extremely superstitious creatures. They didn't so much as take a shit without taking omens first, or interpreting some naturally occurring phenomenon *as* an "omen." The gods spoke in mysterious ways: sometimes you had to call them, sometimes *they* called you. Either way, you checked in with them before you did just about anything.

Liver Spots

The Romans had many ways of reading the gods' minds. Sometimes they would examine the liver of a sacrificial animal and look for spots. Spots were a bad omen. A little advice: if you're buying meat at the local grocery store and you see spots on the meat—*that's* a bad omen. Check out the fish instead.

Bird Watching

Another way the Romans took omens was a process called "augury"— or bird watching. Augury was performed by—you guessed it!— Augurs. An "Augur" was a special kind of priest who was skilled in the ways of our winged friends and who knew how to interpret bird signs. It worked like this: the Augur took his magic stick (called a *lituus,*) and inscribed a big square box in the dirt on the ground, roughly five feet square. Then he divided the box into four equal sections and in one of the boxes on the right side he wrote the word "yes," and in another on the same side he wrote "definitely." On the left side, in one box he wrote "no," and in the other he wrote something like "don't even *think* of parking here!" He then sat cross-legged on the intersection of all four boxes, in the center of the big box, and gazed skyward. In his imagination, he would project the outlines of the box up into the sky. There he would sit and wait and watch until a bird flew through one of the boxes, which would give him his answer. As you can see, this was a system that could, and often did, lead to extreme corruption and manipulation.

The Left-Handed Legion

So this was how the Latin term "sinister" came to mean something "unlucky," or "ill-omened." The Romans were so superstitious about the left side of life that even left-handed people were shunned and segregated in the Roman army. In the Roman army, they took all the left handed soldiers and placed them into a single legion and sent that legion as far away from Rome as possible—all the way to the northernmost boundary of the empire: Hadrian's wall in Scotland. And to this day, if you go to visit the wall, the locals will tell you that the ghosts of the Left-handed Legion still haunt the Scottish moors around the ruins of Hadrian 's Wall.

8) Testicle

You're probably wondering why we didn't deal with this word when we "dissected" the etymology of the human body earlier. It was because this word has such a bizarre story to tell that I didn't want it to "fall through the crack," as it were.

The word "testicle" is made up of the Latin noun *testis*, which means "witness," as in someone who is called into court to give *test*imony in a trial. Once we extract the root *test,* then all we have to do is add the diminutive suffix "cle" onto it. So, literally, a "testicle" is a "little witness." So how does this technically legal term come to be used for a particular part of a man's genitalia? Well, there are two prevailing theories on this, and you'll find that there are as many people who agree with the first as with the second.

Testicle: Theory #1

In ancient Rome, when called to testify at a trial, a witness had to swear an oath that he would tell the truth—similar to our practice today. But because the ancient Romans didn't have a Bible—or any document like it—on which a witness would have to place his hand while he swore his oath *"dicere veritatem, omnen vertitatem, et nihil sed vertitatem,"* it was custom that the witness grab his balls and swear by them. If you think about it, this was a very effective way of ensuring that someone would *dicere* the *veritas* and only the *veritas*, because if it were found out that he had not, he stood the chance of losing something quite near and dear to him!

Testicle: Theory #2

In ancient Rome, since a man's household slaves enjoyed an intimate relationship with their masters—a relationship that often made them privy to their master's comings and goings, when, and with whom— overhearing little things muttered in dark corners meant for ears others than their own—the testimony of a slave could be very powerful stuff in the hands of a wily prosecutor. But many slaves were also quite loyal to their masters, or might be reluctant to testify against them in open court out of fear of repercussions should his master not be convicted. So it was Roman law that a slave could only testify against his master—or *any* member of the household in which he worked, for that matter—if that testimony was extracted under physical torture. This is quite the opposite of the way our legal system works today. Today, any statement given under any force of duress, be it physical or otherwise, is almost always ruled inadmissible, without exception. Not so for the Romans, at least when it came to the testimony of slaves.

It worked like this: the slave was called in and strapped down to the witness chair. Then a court official—usually some big, brawny, mean-faced brute with large muscular hands—would stand next to the slave with one hand under the slave's tunic, gripping the poor fellow's nuts and begin to apply pressure as the questioning began. Then, as the interrogation proceeded, if it was the opinion of the court members that the slave was not forthcoming to their satisfaction, they would give the nod to the man with his "hand on the switch," so to speak, and he would turn up the pressure. A lot of testimony probably went much like this:

Slave: "...I think I heard him say...he wanted to learn to please her..."

SQUEEEEEEEEEEEEEEEZE!

Slave "...I mean I think I heard him say *he wanted to murder Caesar*!"

There is some truth to the old adage—for which this might very well be the origin: When you've got them by the balls, their hearts and minds will follow!

9) The "F" Word

If there are two theories on the history of "testicle," there are probably more than you can count for the etymology of "fuck." Frankly, we're all just guessing.

Grammatically, "fuck" can be anything. It can be a noun ("That was one screaming fuck I got last night!"); or a verb ("I fucked the shit out of that bitch all night long!"); it can be an adjective ("She says he's a virtual fucking machine!"); it can be an adverb ("That's one fucking bad haircut you got today at the mall.);   it need not even *have* sexual connotation ("That's a lot of fucking crap you've got there!"). It can mean something good ("I really got fucked last night!"); or, it can mean something bad ("I really got fucked last night!"); it makes for a great interjection ("Fuck! I can't find my keys!). It also functions well as an interruption ("Outfuckingrageous!" or "I underfuckingestimated what an ass-hole you can be!"). This tells us nothing about the etymology of the word; it is just a commentary on the impressive range of usages the word has acquired over time. To cover all the theories on the history of this word would be to write its own book, which I'm sure has been done, and probably done badly. It would be hard—if even possible—to do it well.

The *Dictionary of American Slang* (1960) gives as the primary meaning of the word: "[taboo] To Cheat, trick, take advantage of, deceive, or treat someone unfairly." It goes on to offer this as an explanation of the relationships between fraud and sex: "All slang meanings of 'fuck' and all 'fuck' expressions, of course, derive consciously or unconsciously from the old and standard but taboo 'fuck' = sexual intercourse. All slang meanings and expressions were widely used in W.W. II military units, became part of the slang vocabulary of many veterans, and spread from them to students and friends. This coupling with the lessening of moral standards and taboos, including linguistic taboos, during and after the war, has contributed to…" blah, blah, blah. To tell you the truth, I have no idea what *any* of that just meant!

From the *New Oxford American Dictionary*, 2nd Edition (2005) we learn that "fuck" came into the English language by slipping through the Indo-European back door and surfacing as the Germanic word *fuk*. It goes on to explain that the word took its derivation from the classical Latin root *pug*, from the verb *pugnare*, which means "to fight"—generally with one's fists, scrapping it out in the dirt, as it were (which can't help but put one in mind of the old Lennon/McCartney song *Why Don't We Do It in the Road*). This is an interesting theory, and we might give it some (though cautious) credence. At the very least, they are correct in that the root of the word "fuck" is classical, but it's not Latin, nor *pug*nacious in any way.

The simple truth is that "fuck"—obviously one of the oldest words in the language—if not the world—dates back to nearly the birth of writing, back when our ancestors were barely up on their feet, still hunting and gathering. It comes from the Greek verb φυω (say: "foo-owe"), and its Greek root is *phu*. It's an agricultural term. It means, literally, to plant seeds—what a farmer does—dropping seeds into a furrow of soil. When adopted by the Romans, its Latin root changed from *phu* to *fu,* and the noun *fututio* soon became part of Roman vernacular.

The "Old In Out"

Fututio is an example of what linguists refer to as a "frequentative." That is, a word that describes repeated action—which is the nature of dropping seeds into a furrow, one after another, after another. It's also a big part of the act of "fucking"—if you're doing it right! It takes often considerable repetition to get those seeds to spurt out. Soon, the Roman elegiac poets got hold of the word at a time when erotic love poetry was all the rage in Rome, and *fututio* became a metaphor for planting a "particular" kind of "seed" in a "specific" kind of "furrow." This literary debauchery—what the *American Dictionary of Slang* calls "linguistic tabooism"—began with Catullus in the first century B.C. and then was taken up by his successors, Propertius, Tibullus and Ovid. When it came to elegy, Ovid was king. Among the many books of poetry that Ovid wrote was one called the *Ars Amatoria* or the *Art of Love*, a poem whose main theme is how to pick up chicks in ancient Rome. It's really a scream, but it, and others like it that came from Ovid's stylus, were considered too vulgar and ultimately offensive to the emperor Augustus (who was certainly not one to preach about promiscuity given his own reputation!), so he had poor Ovid—who at the time was already in his mid fifties—exiled to an army camp on the southern Steppes of Russia by the shores of the Black Sea, where he would spend the rest of his life. You could say this about Augustus— he really *fucked* Ovid!

Fish Story

If you've ever found yourself stuck in traffic or stopped at a red light and noticed that attached somewhere on the rear of the car in front of you is a small chrome fish—more the outline of a fish, quite simple, about six inches long—you probably realize that you know something about the people who own that car: they're "Christians." Because the fish is one of the universal symbols for Jesus. It's not as popular as the cross—hell no, not by a long shot. But if you live in The South— which, for my sins, I happen to—then you see plenty of them. Fish, I mean. On bumpers, that is. Sometimes the word "Jesus" appears inside the little oval shaped body of the fish; sometimes, there is simply a little cross near the front where the eye would be. Often, it is just left blank. A chrome-plated fish, six inches long, stuck onto the back of your car tells the world you've "found Jesus"—or maybe by putting the symbol on the back of your car, you're making it easier for Jesus to find *you*.

Either way, one question remains: why a *fish*? The cross is a no-brainer, but a *fish*? We know it was used as a secret symbol by the Christians to identify each other in public, but still: why a *fucking fish*? There are three theories on this question. Whenever I ask my class about this, I always get some version of the first two—both of which, I'll let you know up front, are incorrect.

Fish: Theory #1

Somewhere in the Bible, there is the account of Jesus feeding the multitudes with two fishes and a few loaves of bread—or was it a few fishes and two loaves of bread? Either way, it went down as one of his "miracles" because basically a "multitude" is a hell of a lot of people, and there just was not very much food to go around—besides, who knew Jesus was a Sushi chef on top of everything else? But somehow, Jesus made everyone happy. It sort of puts one in mind of Woodstock, about day three, after the concert had run too long and all the acid dealers were running out of purple haze and blotter tabs, but somehow, everyone managed to cop a buzz. It was a miracle, really. Maybe it was because Jesus was there as well—certainly plenty of people claim to have *seen* him there!

Fish: Theory #2

Let's not forget that most of Jesus' disciples were fishermen. Out there on the sea of Galilee, one day they were having a hard time getting a nibble until Jesus walked on out there—let me say that again, *walked* on out there—let's face it, it's the only way to go fishing on the Sea of Galilee *without* a boat—and told them to cast their nets "over there." So they cast their nets "over there" and hauled in more fish than they could even carry back. No fools, they realized this guy knew his fishing and maybe they could learn something from him. Hence the term "disciple," whose root, *disc,* comes from the Latin verb *discere,* which means "to teach" as well as "to learn." So these fishermen became Jesus' "disciples" which means they became his "students." The disciples were following Jesus around because they wanted to "learn" how to be better fishermen—asking him questions about bait and nets and tackle and lures until he told them, "Follow me, and I'll make you *fishers of men.*" This wasn't exactly what they had in mind, but what the hell, Jesus had this hot babe with him named Mary and word was for a few sheckles she'd put out.

Fish: Theory #3

It's actually quite simple. The Greek word for fish is ιχθυς (say: "ick-thus"). And the letters of the word form an acronym for Jesus' name and title:

```
ι  χ  θ  υ  ς
η  ρ  ε  ι  ω
σ  ι  ο  ο  τ
υ  σ  υ  ς  η
ς  τ     ρ
   ο
   ς
```

ιησυς = Jesus
χριστος = Christ
θεου = (of) God
υιος = (the) son
σωτηρ = (the) savior

"Jesus Christ, the son of God, the Savior"

Some people ask why they needed the symbol of the fish in the first place. Wasn't the cross enough? That's a problematic issue because the earliest (we think) recorded use of the cross as a religious icon representing Christianity dates to (we think) the 4th century. But cross or no cross, why did the Christians need a "secret symbol" at all? Simple: survival.

The Fire of 64 A.D.

It was during the reign of Nero, in 64 A.D., that one of the worst fires in Rome's history occurred. Like most fires, it began in the vicinity of the Circus Maximus, probably because some old whore knocked over a lamp in her archway brothel while getting the high hard one from a Centurion out on the town and looking to blow a few *denarii* on a tumble in the hay. It lasted for nine days, (the fire, that is—not the tumble) and thanks to the prevailing winds, it spread quickly north, toward the heart of the old city, consuming much of the Imperial Palace on the Palatine Hill as well as many of the buildings and temples of the old Roman Forum in the valley just beyond that, not to mention causing serious damage to much of the architecture of grand Imperial Fora nearby.

Nero, my Hero

Many stories have circulated about Nero and that fire. One was that Nero played the fiddle while Rome burned (actually it would have been a cithara or lyre, as the violin had yet to be invented); another story was that while viewing the conflagration from the terrace of the Imperial Palace, he recited a passage from the second book of the *Aeneid* in which Vergil describes the burning of Troy. This last story is especially hard to believe because Nero's Palace was right in the path of the fire, and knowing Nero, he would have been the first one out the fire exit! There were even rumors that it had been Nero himself who started the fire in order to clear ground for the building of a new imperial residence he had been planning, the famous Domus Aurea, or "Golden House."

The truth is that Nero was not even *in* Rome at the time of the fire, and although he acted quickly in providing emergency shelters for the homeless, and men and resources for the reconstructive efforts, his already waning popularity took a nose dive. Despite the fact that Nero was hundreds of kilometers from Rome when the fire broke out, the inescapable fact of the matter was that it happened on his watch and the *denarius* stopped with him.

So what Nero needed was a scapegoat, and he needed one badly—and quickly—so he launched an "official inquiry" into the cause the of the fire—an obvious sham whose only purpose was to finger somebody—*any*body—to feed to the mob, thereby taking the "heat" of the fire off himself.

He ended up blaming a small, obscure religious cult from the eastern province of Judea whose followers worshiped a man who had gone by the name of "Christ." It was a shrewd move on Nero's part. Rome had always had trouble with the province of Judea—Romans, being polytheists, despised the monotheistic Jews and Christians, who in turn returned the favor—so the Roman mob was quick to embrace the *Christiani* as those who had put their beloved city to the torch. Because the Christians hailed from the province of Judea, Nero dispatched one of his most trusted generals, Vespasian (who would later go on to succeed him as emperor), to Judea to sack Jerusalem as payback.

This marked the beginning of what would become the infamous Roman persecution of the Christians, a systematic, methodical slaughter that was as relentless as it was abominable, and that, once set in motion, would not cease for several centuries. Before the fire, the presence of Christians in Rome was at least tolerated by the Romans enough so that the Christians could perform their devotions openly. In fact, by the first century A.D., Rome was home to dozens of eastern cults, the *Christiani* being simply one of the pack. But after Nero's very public condemnation, the Christians were forced underground—literally—causing them to build the famous catacombs where they could practice their devotions and rituals in relative safety, as well as take refuge in whenever they heard the Praetorian Guard trampling by on their well-groomed steeds in search of fresh lion fodder.

The had good reason to hide, the Christians did, for if caught, terrible fates awaited them. One of Nero's favorite forms of torture and execution was to crucify Christians at major intersections throughout the city and then at night set them on fire to amuse drunken Roman aristocrats while helping them find their way through the dark city streets as they caroused from party to party. Thousands were also martyred in the Circus Maximus as well, many more there, in fact, than ever were in the Colosseum—once it was built some fifty years later (a fact not widely known).

Nero did not confine his cruelty to the Christians. Some of Nero's "greatest hits" include the murder of his mother, Agrippina, whom he had his freedman, Anicetus, club to death in her home after a botched attempt at doing the "wet work" himself—literally. One spring day, Nero planned a little picnic for himself and his mother on his private yacht. The plan was a complicated little venture involving a false bottom and a tent with roof beams that should have collapsed but *did not*. Even when you're emperor, you cannot expect to have everything go your way all of the time.

Still, tough as she was (she reportedly swam over a mile to shore following the fiasco on the yacht) Agrippina simply had to go as she had been interfering with Nero's plans to divorce his first wife, Octavia, in order to marry his latest mistress, Poppaea Sabina.

Now, with his mother finally out of the picture, love found a way and he married Poppaea in the year 63 A.D., only to murder her two years later by kicking her to death while she was five months pregnant with their second child. You could write a book about the black reign of Nero (that happens to be a pun, by the way, but it only works in Italian.), and many have been, beginning with the Roman biographer Suetonius, who was born in the year 70 A.D., two years after Nero committed suicide on 9 June, 68 A.D. Nero reigned for only fourteen years—but hey, it was fun while it lasted.

So, back to the Christians and our fish. Naturally, the Christians avoided public gatherings in large groups, and were often terrified of even showing their faces on the open street for fear of being found out. So in order to identify themselves to each other in public, one Christian would draw half of the outline of the symbol of a fish in the dirt with the edge of his sandal, and if the man next to him completed the image, then they knew they were among friends. It was sort of their version of a "secret handshake," as it were.

The Great Perhaps

CHAPTER

15

Survival Tactics

Let's face it. When it comes right down to it, the most important concern to an individual is his own survival. We would not have lasted very long were we not endowed with what we refer to as a "survival instinct." It is not our only instinct, but without it, the others would hardly matter. The word "instinct" derives from the Latin verb *instinguere,* which means to "arouse" or "excite." The idea is that it is your instincts—particularly your *survival* instincts—that keep you alert and, hopefully then, alive.

The End of the Line

We are now at the end of our journey through the *Words of the Day,* the term we have used to investigate the sounds we make and the meanings we assign to them in order to get through the day—to survive. It's not as easy as it looks, you know—survival. Back when Caveman walked the earth, he rarely walked alone. He teamed up with other cavemen to form tribes. This was a highly competitive time in the history of our species, and survival depended on so many different things—the ability to make tools and weapons that enabled us to hunt and eat was only one—but it was a *big* one.

Weapons were developed not only for offense but also for defense—to enable one tribe to protect its "turf" from invasion by another tribe. But spears and flints and clubs and knives weren't the only weapons early man created. Language was also such a "weapon" perhaps the most important of them all. For even though the range of sounds that the human voice can produce is limited, the possible meanings of the sounds are boundless. Therefore, each tribe developed its own meanings for the various sounds they made, and these meanings were guarded secrets, known only to them, so that if they encountered a hostile tribe hot for their turf and it was time to rumble, the members of one tribe wouldn't be able to understand what the members of the other tribe were saying to each other when the shit started to fly, even though the grunts and sounds they made were probably very similar.

Green Right—Hut! Hut!

Sports often preserve many remnants of this age old human survival tactic. Take football, for example. When the quarterback of one of the teams calls the signals before the snap, he may very well be using some of the same words the quarterback of the other team just used, or is going to use, only "Green right! Green right! On three! Hut! Hut!" will mean something different each time. Plus, right doesn't always have to mean "right" if you decide it means "left" in the huddle before the play. And since surprise is always an advantage in every conflict, language is a "weapon" of stealth that can provide that very important edge. This is perhaps one of the main reasons why different languages developed around the world.

But even in countries where the same language is spoken by all, this survival instinct still persists. Once you've got an instinct, it's hard to get rid of it. We all have our crowds, factions, cliques—call them what you will—with whom we share a language that is hybrid and exclusive to outsiders. To be let into a group is to be let into its "jargon"—a word of unknown origin, but which the *New Oxford American Dictionary*, 2nd Edition (2005) defines as "Special words or expressions used by a particular profession or group and are difficult for others to understand." Again, it seems like such schoolyard stuff, but it goes on and has gone on ever since the world began to spin.

For this reason alone, the impossibility of keeping up with the morphing of words makes writing books such as this one seem almost "Sisyphean" in nature. (If you didn't get that last allusion, don't worry, we'll get to Sisyphus in a minute.) All one can do is take a "snapshot," as it were, of the language as it was at that moment in time. So as we wrap this up and take that final journey down into The Underworld, I realize that by the time this book hits the shelves, it will already have become in some ways obsolete. But because the focus of this study has been *not* on how words are currently being used—which *will* change and change again, trust me—but on the classical origins of these words and what *they* meant at the inception of language, it does have considerable validity that will allow it to remain timeless. *Those*, fortunately, will *not* change. So we can at least take some small spoonful of solace in that. But just as you've got to start somewhere, eventually, you have to end somewhere. So let's conclude with a brief look at how the ancient Greeks and Romans viewed *The End*.

The Underworld

Most societies have a vision of an "afterlife." Or an idea that there is something waiting on the other side. It is because we can't contemplate the idea of "nothingness"—that one day we will cease to be. It is a place the mind cannot go. Therefore, we invent places so we can carry around in our heads a mental picture of what might await us—places we call "Heaven" and "Hell" or, in the words of Francois Rabelais, "The Great Perhaps."

Hades

Contrary to popular belief, "Hades" refers not to a place, but to a person. Hades (whose name means "The Unseen") was a god and the ruler of the dead. He was the son of Cronos, which made him the brother of Zeus and Poseidon. When they were splitting up the big pie, as it were, Zeus got to be ruler of the sky, Poseidon got to be ruler of the sea, and Hades got The Underworld. It was a dirty job, but somebody had to do it, and it never seemed to bother old Hades. Better to be king of *something*, he figured. Although Achilles, who was not at all pleased with his accommodations in The Underworld, commented upon his arrival: "Better to be the slave of a poor man on Earth than king among the dead." But as we've seen, Achilles had some issues, tended to be a bit on the moody side, and in general was a hard chap to please.

Death Ancient Style

In classical antiquity, when you died you were escorted to The Underworld by the god Hermes (if you were a Greek), or Mercury (if you were a Roman). Other than that, the view of the afterlife was pretty much the same for both cultures. As we have seen, except for the names of the gods, both cultures shared many of their customs and beliefs. Now, it was down in The Underworld that you would spend the rest of eternity. Most souls spent their time in a sort of grey, bloodless existence, acting out robotically whatever it was they had done in their lives as mortals. As we shall see, this must have been particularly difficult since they no longer had any memory of what it was that they *had* done on Earth as mortals! It was also here than many paid for the crimes that they had committed during their lives on Earth—particularly those who had transgressed against the gods, who, as we saw with Tantalus in Chapter Eight, were very creative in designing their punishments. Each one was tailored in some bizarre way to fit the crime(s) of the particular transgressor.

Lethe

When you arrived in The Underworld, there were some specific procedures you had to follow. First, there were two rivers down there you had to cross—Lethe and the Styx—to get to your final destination, which was—unless some special fate awaited you—the Plain of Asphodel, a dreary place where nothing fun ever happened.

Ancient Brainwashing

You crossed Lethe first because Lethe was the River of Forgetfulness, and to the ancient imagination, the idea of spending eternity in as gloomy a place as The Underworld with any memory of your past life as a mortal—looking upon the blessed light of the sun and enjoying all of the Earthly, carnal pleasures—was just too upsetting and horrifying a prospect to bear. So when crossing the River Lethe, you drank from its waters, and by doing so, all recollection of your former life on earth was washed from your memory.

Lethargic

It is from the river Lethe that we get the much misunderstood and misused word "lethargic." Consulting, yet again, our *Oxford American Dictionary*, we find the definition for "lethargic" as being "sluggish" or "apathetic." This is how most people use the word—to describe a feeling best captured by the word "blah." This is simply not so. Deriving from the word Lethe, the River of Forgetfulness, if you are feeling "lethargic," you are not feeling "sluggish," or "tired," or "blah." You are feeling "forgetful." It is also from the river Lethe that we get the word "lethal." Now, literally, both "lethargic" and "lethal," being adjectives and built on the same root, must mean the same thing. Though it doesn't require much of a leap of imagination to see how "lethal" came to be used for something that "causes death," or is "characteristic of death," because the only way to get to the river Lethe is to die. But technically—literally—etymologically—both words must mean the same thing and that is "forgetful."

Styx

After crossing the River Lethe and drinking from its waters—which each soul had to do on his or her own—you were ferried across the Styx by the ferryman, Charon. For this service, he charged a fare, generally two *obols* which, hopefully, your relatives placed on your corpse, one coin over each of your eyes before burning your body. If they didn't, Charon probably made you swim. When you got to the other side, you had to face a panel of three judges: Minos, Rhadamanthys, and Aeacus. But for most souls, this was a "pro forma" exercise and nothing much really went down. If you think about it, having already crossed the River Lethe and lost all memory of what you did up in the light, how could any meaningful Q&A take place? But for some unlucky souls, things sometimes did get sticky, and if that happened, even though you had forgotten everything yourself, the gods certainly had *not*. In this case, you had to plead for their "amnesty."

Amnesty

When I present this word to my class and ask them what it means, they usually find it a concept extremely difficult to put into words. I can always tell when my students are unsure about a word, because they tend to equivocate when answering ("It means, like...uh..."). Usually, they wind up uttering something along the lines of "mercy" or "forgiveness." They're resorting to what they think the word means based on how they've heard it used—and so have been using it themselves. It's like a knee-jerk reaction that kicks in before their brains have a chance to look at the *ingredients*!

This I illustrate to them by writing the cognate "amnesia" next to "amnesty" and asking them what *that* words means. This time they all immediately respond—correctly, I happily add—"loss of memory." Now they all agree that the words "amnesty" and "amnesia" look quite similar and are obviously made up of the same ingredients. What we have here in both cases is the Greek root *mne* from the verb *mimnesko* (μιμνεσκω—say: mih-mneh-sko) which means "to forget." By now you should be able to recognize the other ingredient, namely the "alpha privative," which negates the root. So, the two words share the same prefix and same root. Therefore—like "lethargic" and "lethal"—they *must* mean the same thing, the only difference possibly being the suffix, which merely determines part of speech. But in this case, even the suffixes mean the same thing. All words in English that end in "ty" are nouns, just as all words in English that end in "ia" are also nouns. So, if all three ingredients are the same, how can "amnesty" mean anything other than what "amnesia" means? Literally, it *cannot*. Therefore, if you are granted "amnesty," then whatever it is you have done has not been "forgiven," but "forgotten." There's a big difference! If you were to arrive home early from work one day and find your wife balling the plumber on the kitchen table, you might find it in your heart one day to "forgive" her, but I doubt you'd ever "forget" it.

Sisyphus

For some of the poor souls who faced the panel of judges on the other side of the Styx, things didn't always go so well. For those people who had really pissed off the gods while living out their mortal lives, "amnesty" was *not* granted. The gods were *not* about to suffer a sudden case of "amnesia." In Chapter Eight, we saw what happened to Tantalus once he got down to The Underworld. Tantalus had invited the gods to a banquet at his house and then butchered his son and fed them the flesh to see if they really were as on the ball as everyone said. Unfortunately for Tantalus, they were. So for *his* punishment, he was forced to spend eternity in a state of extreme hunger and thirst, standing in a cool, fresh water stream that came up to his chin and with a fruit tree full of fruit hanging just over his head. But every time he reached up to grab a piece of fruit, a strong, sudden breeze would blow the boughs out of his reach; and whenever he bent down to have a drink from the stream, it would instantly dry up before he could taste a single drop.

Sisyphus, although known for his cleverness, hadn't the sense to know what any fisherman will tell you: if a fish just kept his mouth shut, he'd never get caught. Well, one day, Sisyphus spots Zeus doing what he did best. This time he was making off with the river nymph Aegina, daughter of the river god Aesopus. Zeus carried her off to the island of Oenone where he whipped out his "one-eyed wonder worm" and let her have it. Aesopus, being the protective father that he was, gave chase and asked Sisyphus which way they went. Sisyphus, known for his cleverness, wasn't about to rat out Zeus unless there was a little something in it for himself. Since Aesopus was a river god, Sisyphus' options were limited, so he asked for—get this—a spring of fresh water. This was no problem for a river god like Aesopus, who then got from Sisyphus the information he needed to track down Zeus and try to save his daughter.

Zeus was so pissed off at Sisyphus for ratting him out that he summoned Thanatos, the god of death, to take him down to the House of Hades. But Sisyphus, known for his cleverness, outwitted Thanatos and ended up living out his life in ease and luxury on earth. But the gods never forget a wrong—no sudden "amnesia" or "amnesty" for them! And when it came time for Sisyphus to cross the Styx and be judged, they were "expecting" him…

Get it up there, Sisyphus!

The special punishment that Zeus devised for Sisyphus was that for all of eternity his soul was forced to push this huge boulder up a steep hill with the knowledge that if he could get it up and over the other side, he would be freed from his torment. But what he did *not* know was that each time he got the boulder close to the top of the hill, it was destined to roll back down again. And each time it rolled back down, thinking that one more time might be the charm, he would be destined to try again. And again. And again. Hence, we refer to a task that is futile, impossible or never-ending, as "Sisyphean."

Famous Last Words

As he lay dying, it was reported that Oscar Wilde's last words were, "Either that wallpaper goes, or I do." Thoreau, when asked on his deathbed whether or not he had made peace with his maker, is said to have replied, "I was not aware we had quarreled." We'd all like to end our lives on a punch line, with a real zinger. Sadly, most of us don't. Most of us leave the world much the way we entered it: terrified, screaming and crying. The best we can hope for is to go down like the Mexican outlaw Pancho Villa, who, as legend has it, uttered with his last, dying breath, "Please...don't let it end like this. Tell them I said *something.*"